The Wolf Marshall Guitar Method
Basics 1
A Complete Guide To Mastering The Guitar
By Wolf Marshall
The Visual System Of Learning Guitar

CONTENTS

 **HAL•LEONARD® CORPORATION**

7777 W. BLUEMOUND RD. P.O. BOX 13819 MILWAUKEE, WI 53213

Wolf Marshall

Born in New York City, New York, Wolf Marshall was inundated with musical sounds at an early age. He was raised in Los Angeles, CA in a musical household — his mother a classical pianist and his uncle, a violinist. By 15, he had gone through violin, piano and cello lessons and moved on to electric guitar. Wolf turned pro at 16, performing in rock clubs and concert halls throughout the Los Angeles and Southland area. Shortly thereafter, he entered college with the intention of marrying his rock, blues and jazz interests with a bonafide classical background. While in school, he worked the L.A. session scene and began transcribing music for jazz giant and mentor Pat Martino. After graduating from UCLA with a degree in Music Theory and Composition, Wolf went on to apply his considerable knowledge, expertise and performing abilities to modern pedagogy.

With more than 60 instructional works — transcription books, audio cassettes, CDs, videos and other study aids — and countless magazine articles and columns to his credit, Wolf is considered by his peers and the many who follow his teaching to be the contemporary authority in his field. Serving as a guitar expert to top players, teachers and students alike, his contributions and impact on the area of modern guitar instruction are unequaled.

Now, harnessing his many years of playing, writing and teaching experience, this celebrated performing educator brings it all together for you in this long-waited series, the Wolf Marshall Guitar Method.

Introduction

With Basics 1 you'll launch straight into a hands-on contemporary approach to learning both the foundations of guitar and music. The essential visual elements of shapes and patterns on the guitar fretboard unlock the secret to successful and creative playing. From the moment you first touch the fingerboard, tune up the guitar and play your first chord — you are a guitarist!

You'll learn exciting power chords shapes, strum patterns, riffs patterns, guitar techniques like muting and string bending. All presented with contemporary music examples and figures (from rockabilly to hard rock). In addition, you'll gain essential musical knowledge from the basics of notation, (including tablature and grids) rhythm and meter and intervals to transposition. Special Playing Tips and Music Builders sections further enhance your guitar and music chops.

You'll also learn the basics of blues playing and unveil the mysteries of the 12-bar progression and, with it, the blues-rock connection.

Please note that there is a complete listing of all the products in the Wolf Marshall Method at the very end of this book.

Foreword

To develop a new guitar method is an ambitious project. To come up with something that is different, meaningful and contemporary is even more so.

The method is actually the result of years of practical experience, observations and insights gained through contact with numerous guitar giants, countless transcriptions of actual music, analysis and feedback from students and teachers in the educational environment. Through these means, a number of vital basic concepts, rooted in solid fretboard dynamics, revealed themselves. You could say that the fruits of the labor of a vast number of musicians contributed to the material in the formative stages. Inevitably, the logic presented itself — a way of looking at the instrument and getting to the music waiting to be played.

The Wolf Marshall method is committed to training the ear — that primary apparatus of music. The goal is to coordinate and maximize the ear/hand relationship and unite this with a player's mind and, most important, their feel. These comprise the art of guitar music.

Through the use of the unique music-tab-grid system of the Wolf Marshall method, a player can tie together the various important aspects of physical technique, fretboard visualization and mastery, functional theory and harmonic knowledge with ear training.

The Wolf Marshall Method is about training your hands and ear simultaneously to liberate what you hear in your head and make it happen on the fingerboard. It's about removing blockages, it's about ideas for both improvising and writing. But most of all, it's about enjoying guitar playing so much that you will want to pick it up often and not set it down until you drop.

Wolf Marshall

Also Available....
Supplemental Songbooks To Go Along With Your Wolf Marshall Method!
Containing The Songs You Want To Play
Divided Into Sections That Correlate To Each Chapter In Each Book!

"Power Songs One"
For Use With "Basics One"
"Power Songs Two"
For Use With "Basics Two"
"Power Songs Three"
For Use With "Basics Three"
"Power Songs Four"
For Use With "Advanced Concepts And Techniques"

These songbooks include songs by The Police, The Beatles, Derek And The Dominos, Stevie Ray Vaughan, Eric Clapton, U2, Aerosmith, Hendrix, The Who, Kiss, Allman Brothers, Ozzy Osbourne, Pink Floyd, Free, Cinderella, Van Morrison, Kinks, Bon Jovi, B.B. King, Billy Joel, Elvis Presley, Lynyrd Skynyrd and more!

All Four Books Include a Special Bonus Section listing additional songs that can be used with each chapter. Included are Van Halen, Led Zeppelin, Jeff Healy, Joe Satriani, Robert Cray, Tom Petty, Eagles, ZZ Top, Creedence Clearwater Revival, Neil Young, Deep Purple, Metallica, Guns 'N' Roses and many more!

Available In Book And Book/Audio Formats!
See Back Inside Cover Of This Book For Ordering Information!

ESSENTIAL INFORMATION

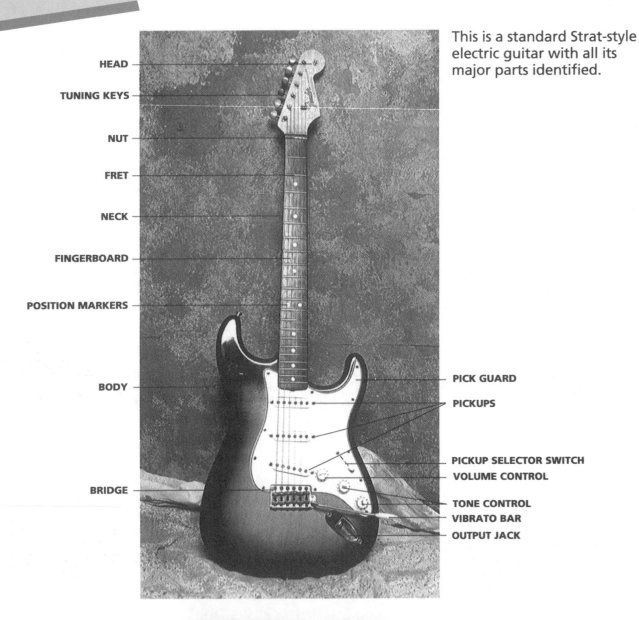

This is a standard Strat-style electric guitar with all its major parts identified.

HEAD
TUNING KEYS
NUT
FRET
NECK
FINGERBOARD
POSITION MARKERS
BODY
BRIDGE

PICK GUARD
PICKUPS
PICKUP SELECTOR SWITCH
VOLUME CONTROL
TONE CONTROL
VIBRATO BAR
OUTPUT JACK

A standard electric or acoustic guitar has six strings. Each is tuned to a different pitch as follows:

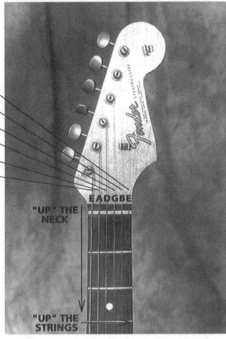

1st string = E ("high E")
2nd string = B
3rd string = G
4th string = D
5th string = A
6th string = E ("low E")

EADGBE

"UP" THE NECK

"UP" THE STRINGS

The direction of motion on the guitar is referred to in terms of *pitch* (how high or low a note sounds.) Thus, motion *up* the neck is motion moving away from the nut and toward the bridge, and motion *up* the strings is motion moving away from the sixth string and toward the first string. Motion *down* the strings or neck proceeds in the opposite directions.

BASIC TECHNIQUE

This photo shows a correct standing posture for playing the guitar, including basic right and left hand positionings.

This photo shows a correct sitting posture for playing the guitar. Notice that legs and right arm, or strap and right arm support the guitar. The left arm is not used for support.

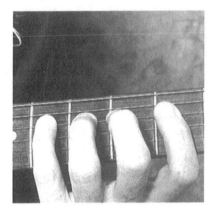

The left hand should hold the neck from underneath with the fingers laying lightly on the strings and the thumb centered behind the neck. Only the thumb and fingers should touch the neck. The left hand should not be supporting the neck.

The palm of the picking hand should rest lightly on the bridge with the underside of the forearm resting on the front of the guitar body.

Hold your pick as shown and attack the low E string. Keep the motion small enough that it stops before you strike the A string.

This is called a *downstroke*.

TUNING THE GUITAR

1. Tuning To The Recording
If you have the accompanying cassette tape or CD, you can tune to track one of the recording.

When you are tuning the guitar, you will adjust the pitch (highness or lowness of sound) of each string by turning the corresponding tuning key. Tightening a string raises the pitch and loosening it lowers the pitch.

3. Tuning To A Keyboard
If you have a piano or keyboard, you can easily tune each string as shown:

2. Electronic Guitar Tuner
If you have a electronic guitar tuner, you can easily tune your guitar by following the instructions that came with the tuner.

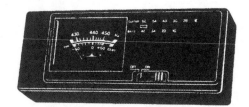

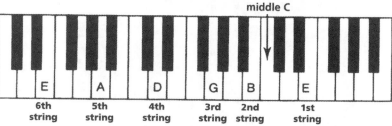

middle C

E	A	D	G	B	E
6th string	5th string	4th string	3rd string	2nd string	1st string

4. Relative Tuning
To tune your guitar by ear, you must tune the strings to each other. This is done in the following manner:

Assuming that the sixth string is tuned correctly to E, press the 6th string behind the 5th fret. Play the depressed 6th string and the open 5th string together. When the two sounds match, you are in tune.

Press the 5th string behind the 5th fret and tune the open 4th string to it. Follow the same procedure that you did on the 5th and 6th strings.

Press the 4th string behind the 5th fret and tune the open 3rd string to it.

To tune the 2nd string, press the 3rd string behind the 4th fret and tune the open 2nd string to it.

Press the 2nd string behind the 5th fret and tune the 1st string to it.

Guitar strings sometimes slip out of tune, so it never hurts to double check your tuning.

GUITAR AND MUSIC NOTATION

Guitar music can be notated three different ways: on a *musical staff*, in *tablature* and on a *grid*. All three formats are used throughout this course to illustrate the various concepts introduced. The following is a brief overview of each system.

The Musical Staff

The musical staff shows pitches and rhythms and is divided by *bar lines* into *measures*.

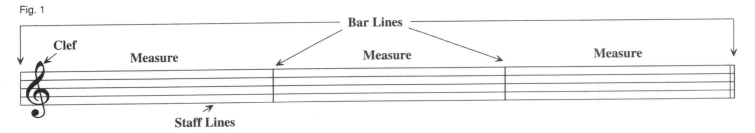

Fig. 1

Measures are commonly divided into four, evenly-spaced *beats*, indicated by the *time signature* "4/4". The beats provide a point of reference for communicating different rhythms. Counting "**one**, two, three, four, **one**, two, three, four" with an emphasis on "one" enables us to keep track of the beats and measures.

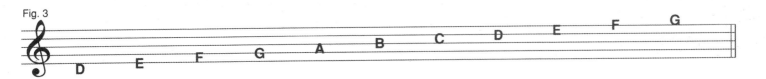

Fig. 2

Each *line* on the staff represents a different pitch, as do the *spaces* between the lines. Pitches are named after the first seven letters of the alphabet (A, B, C, D, E, F and G).

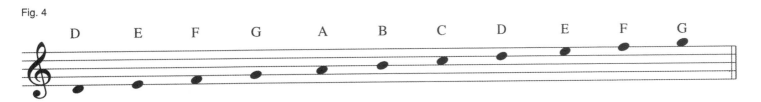

Fig. 3

Noteheads are placed on the lines or in the spaces to indicate what pitch to play.

Fig. 4

Unusually high and low pitches are indicated by placing noteheads on *ledger lines* above and below the staff.

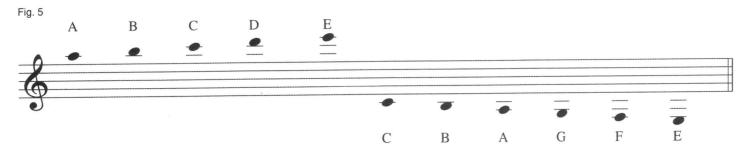

Fig. 5

Tablature

Tablature shows locations on the fretboard and is also divided by bar lines into measures. Each of tablature's six horizontal lines represents one string on the guitar.

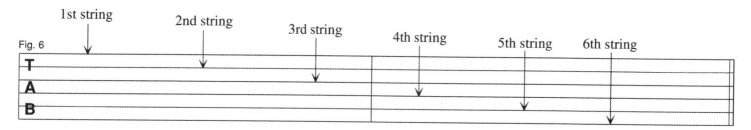

Fret numbers are placed on the lines to indicate exact "fretboard coordinates". For example, "3rd fret/6th string" would be indicated by a "3" on the bottom line.

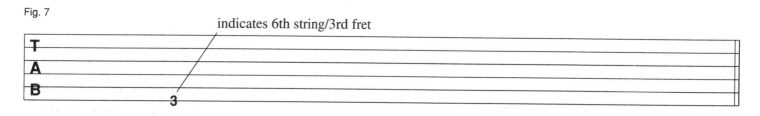

Open strings are indicated by zeros.

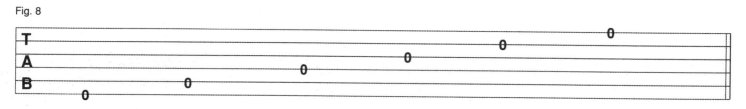

Tablature usually appears directly below a musical staff notating the same music, the numbers in the tablature corresponding to the notes directly above them on the staff.

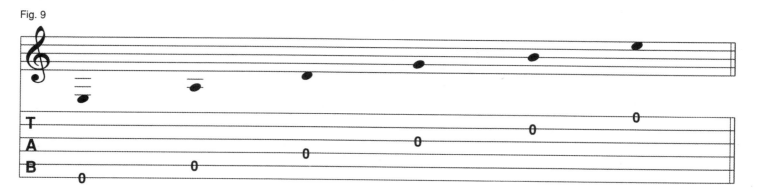

Used in this format, tablature (or "tab") is an invaluable aid for learning to read music on the guitar.

The Grid

The grid provides a strong visual image of the fretboard; the vertical lines represent the strings and the horizontal lines represent the frets. The top line represents the nut, unless otherwise indicated. The grid not only depicts the strings and frets visually but also what the notes are. Note names are added to the Grid to explore the musical geography of the fingerboard.

Note names are shown on the grid.

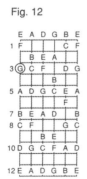

Fig. 12

Circles are superimposed onto the grid to show fretted notes.

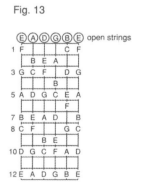

Fig. 13

Open strings are indicated by hollow circles above the nut.

When combined with musical notation on the staff and tablature, a powerful visual tool is created. The fretted notes are circled in the grids and important musical points are further highlighted in color, presenting clear physical and mental guitar pictures. Color is also used purposefully to highlight and emphasize important points in the staff and tablature of the musical examples.

Chapter 1

**POWER CHORDS
TWO NOTE POWER CHORDS**

Look at these three chords.

E5   A5   D5

Playing Tip

To fret a note in any one of these chords, press the tip of your left index finger firmly onto the string, **behind** the 2nd fret, not on it.

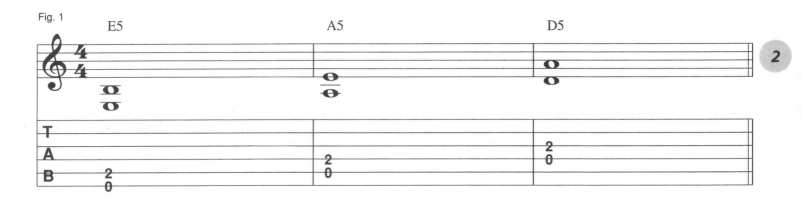

Fig. 1

Play each open power chord by strumming the two strings with a single downstroke. To do this, allow the pick to glide across both strings in the chord, but do not allow the pick to strike any other strings.

These are the same simple, but useful, open power-chord forms used extensively in rock, blues, metal and pop and are found in the music of AC/DC, Aerosmith, Stevie Ray Vaughn, Van Halen, the Beatles and countless others.

The Chord Shapes

Looking at the grids in the following figure, notice the similarity in shape from one chord to the next:

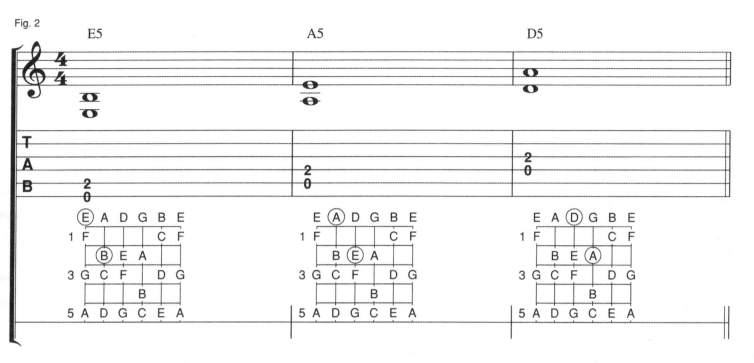

These are *power chords* and are *two-note voicings*. For example, A + E = A5: it gets its name from the first step *(root)* A and fifth step *(fifth)* E. The "steps" or distance between two notes is known as an *interval*. The following chart illustrates this idea.

Step #:	1	2	3	4	5	6	7	8
Note Name:	A	B	C	D	E	F	G	A
Step Name:	Root				5th			

Notice the root is the open string in all three chords.

COUNTING RHYTHM

The division of music into regular units of time (measures) is called *meter*. Meter is indicated on the staff by the *time signature* (see Fig. 3 below). A pattern of four beats in a measure is called *common time*. It is represented in the time signature by 4/4 as shown below in Fig. 3.

Fig. 3

Time Signature

count: "one, two, three, four, one, two, three, four, one, two, three, four."

beats: 1 2 3 4   1 2 3 4   1 2 3 4

Each beat takes up the same amount of time. None of the beats should be longer or shorter that any other. Remembering to count evenly, begin counting "**one**, two, three, four, **one**, two, three, four," etc. Make sure that you count "one" a little louder than the other beats to help you feel the division of the music into measures. The first beat in a measure is referred to as the *downbeat*.

Fig. 4

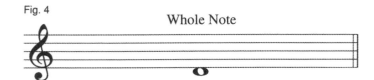

Whole Note

This is a whole note. It is held for four beats.

Begin counting "**one**, two, three, four," even and steady. Now, strum the E5 chord at the same time you count "**one**" and let the chord ring as you count "two, three, four." Next, strum the E5 again and hold it for four more beats. Repeat this pattern two more times.

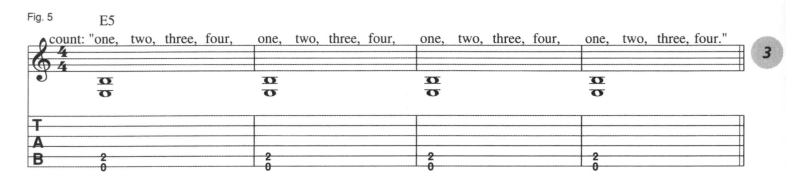

Again, begin counting "**one**, two, three, four," even and steady. Now, strum the E5 chord at the same time you count "**one**" and let it ring for four beats. Next, strum the A5 as you count "one" and hold it for four beats. Repeat this pattern two more times. When you can switch these chords quickly and smoothly, there should not be any silence as you switch from one to another. Switching chords is known as a *chord change*.

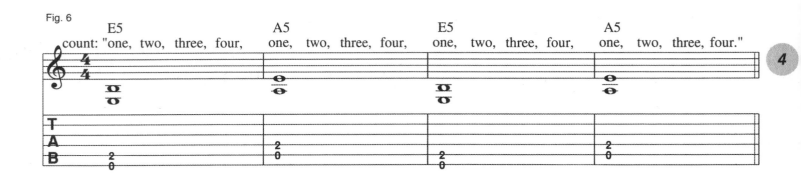

You have just played a very simple four-bar phrase in 4/4 meter using whole-note rhythms.

Let's play another four-bar phrase that uses the E5-A5-D5 *chord progression* (also referred to simply as a *progression*). Remember to keep your beats steady and even, to hold each chord for its entire four counts, and to change chords as quickly as possible as you get to the next downbeat.

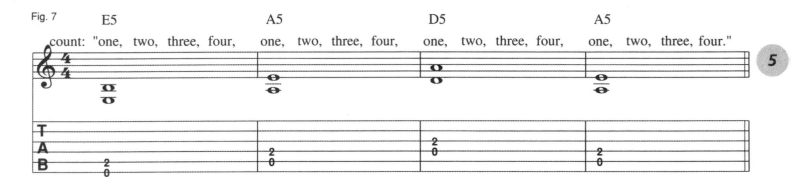

Now, let's divide the whole-note rhythm into *half notes* . This is the symbol for a half note.

Fig. 8   Half Note

It gets held for two beats. (Two half notes take up the same amount of time as one whole note.)

In the following figure, strum on **"one"** and **"three,"** letting each half note ring for two beats. Be sure that you strum at exactly the same time that you speak each count. Notice that the *feel* of the half note rhythm pattern is different from the the feel of the whole-note rhythm pattern.

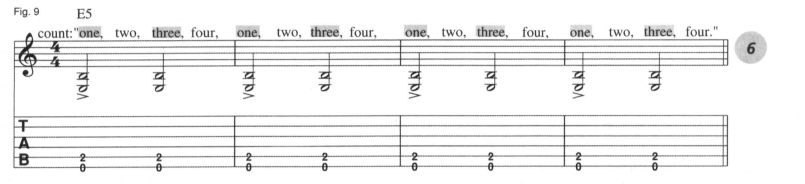

Fig. 9   E5

Notice the *accent mark* in this figure. It indicates a note that is to be played (and counted) a little louder than the other notes. Here, we are accenting the downbeat in order to emphasize the start of each new measure. This is the same idea you were working on when you learned to count time and counted each **"one"** a little louder than you counted "two-three-four".

Next, strum E5 on beat 1, hold it for two beats, then change to A5 on beat 3 and hold it for two beats. Play the accented notes slightly louder than the others. Do this several times.

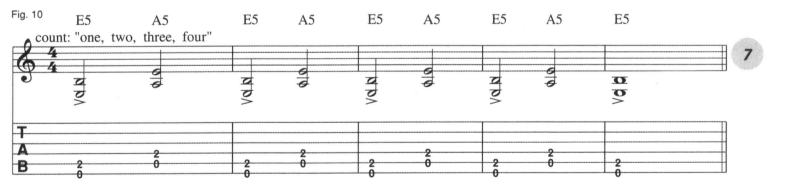

Fig. 10

Play slowly, accurately and with steady timing.

Now apply the same idea to the A5-D5 and E5-A5-D5 progressions.

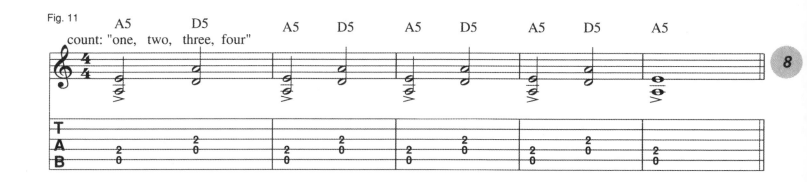

Fig. 11

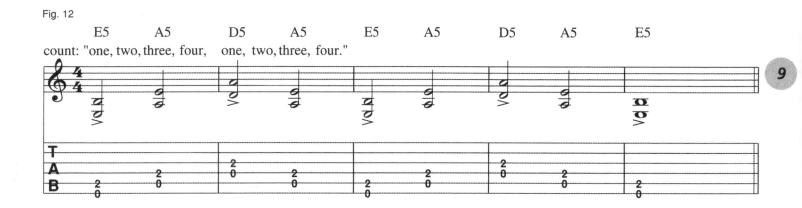

Fig. 12

By dividing a measure of 4/4 meter into four equal parts, we get four *quarter notes* — one for each beat. (Four quarter notes equal two half notes, or one whole note.) This is the symbol for a quarter note.

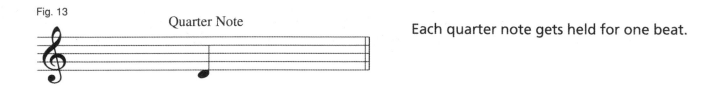

Fig. 13

Quarter Note

Each quarter note gets held for one beat.

Using all downstrokes, strum the E5 chord in a quarter-note rhythm.

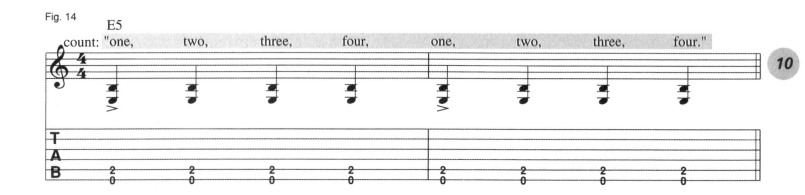

Fig. 14

Now try changing from E5 to A5 to D5 power chords using a quarter-note rhythm. Proceed slowly and strive for a smooth change between each chord while maintaining a steady meter. Notice once again that the quarter-note rhythm is different in feel than the half-note and whole-note rhythms.

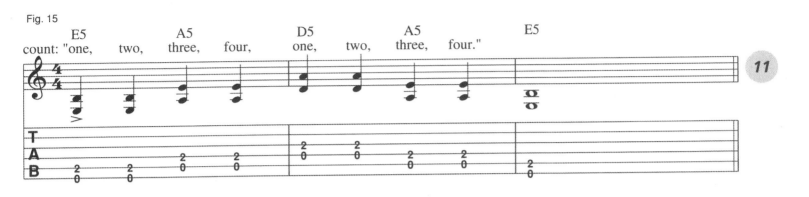

Fig. 15

Playing Tip

Before you start to play the following progression, try to do the following:

1. Tap your foot instead of counting out loud (but continue to count mentally).
2. Tap your foot on each beat as you tap out the rhythms with your hand.
3. Accent the downbeat by tapping it a bit louder than the other beats.
4. Always maintain a steady and even count. This is called maintaining a steady *tempo*. Tempo refers to how fast or slow you play.

Once you start playing the following progressions, try to do the following:

Practice slowly until you can play even, relaxed and accurate. Then gradually work up to faster speeds or tempos.

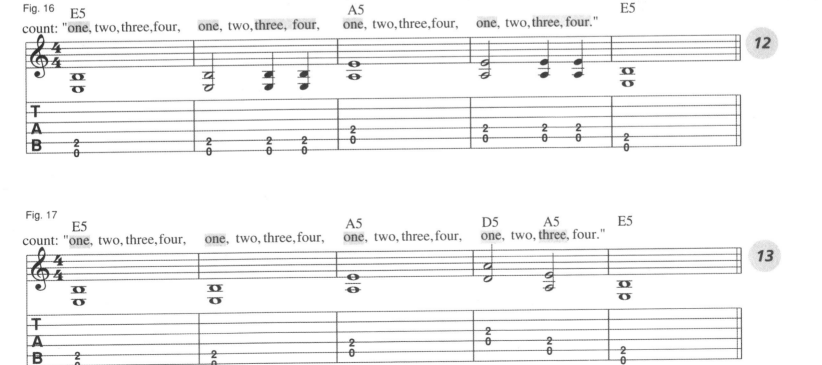

Fig. 16

Fig. 17

THREE NOTE POWER CHORDS

Let's expand our open power chords into *three-note voicings*. Using A5 as an example, a three-note voicing is formed by *doubling* the root (A) one octave higher. In this case, the chord remains an A5 chord, but it sounds thicker (or fuller) than the two-note A5 chord.

Step #	**1**	2	3	4	**5**	6	7	**1**(8)
Note Name:	**A**	B	C	D	**E**	F	G	**A**
Step Name:	**Root**				**5th**			**Octave**

Here are the open E5 and A5 power chords in three-note form.

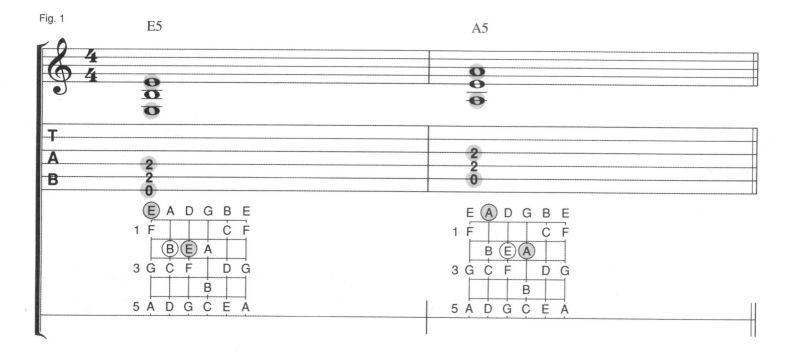

As before, each chord's root is on an open string. The index finger is flattened out and used to fret the top two notes.

This technique is known as *barring*. Barring is indicated on the grid by an arch which connects the two hollow circles that represent the notes.

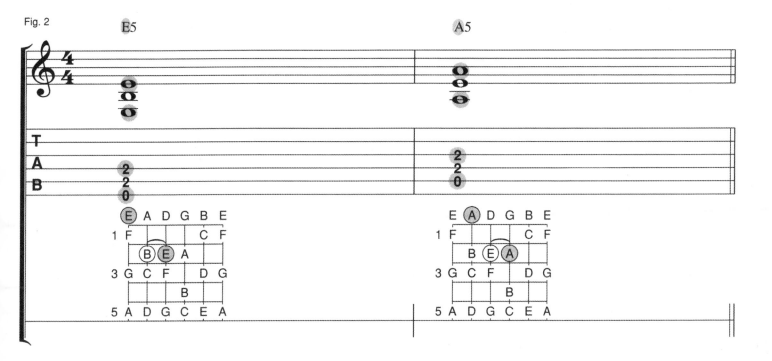

When barring, press the index finger down firmly enough to produce a clear, buzz-free sound. Strum the open, three-note E5 and A5 chords now.

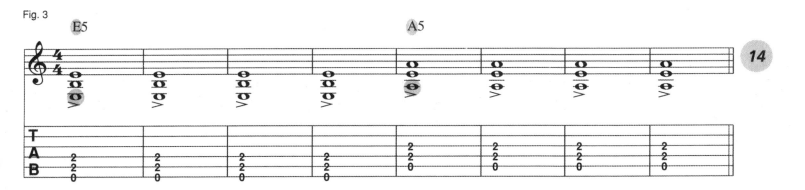

Practice the chord change between the open E5 and A5 power chords in whole-note rhythm to get a feel for changing three-note chords and barring.

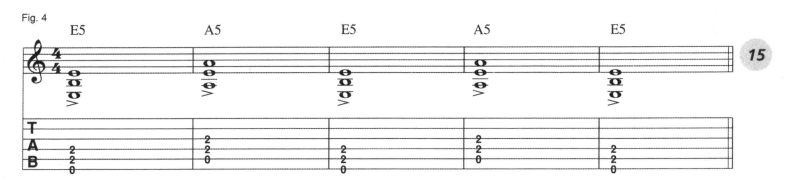

The open D5 chord in three-note form involves using the 4th, 3rd and 2nd strings. Its fingering shape is different than that employed for the open E5 and A5 chords, requiring two fingers.

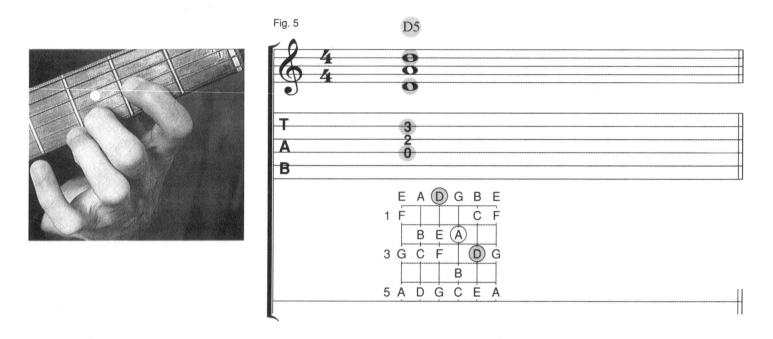

Fig. 5

Playing Tip

Strum this shape making sure to avoid the 5th and 6th strings.

The following progression employs the open, three-note power chords introduced above in a steady quarter-note rhythm with a chord change every bar.

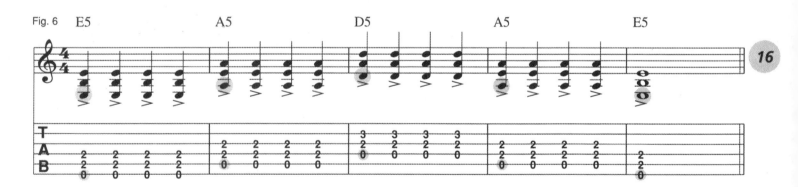

Here's another progression to play. This one utilizes whole notes and half notes in 4/4 meter.

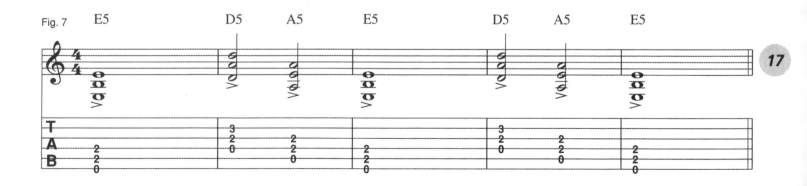

These are the progressions from Chapter One in three-note form. These will provide both valuable review and reinforcement.

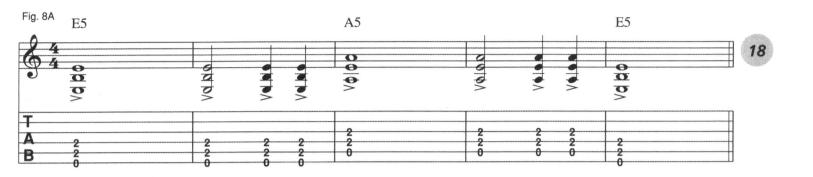

Fig. 8A

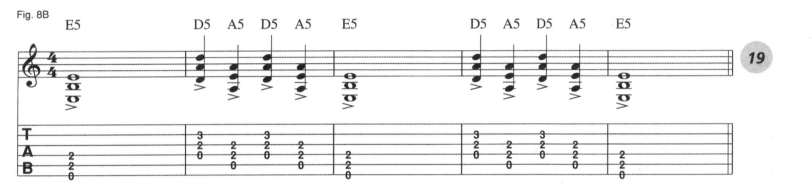

Fig. 8B

EIGHTH NOTES

This is the symbol for a single eighth note.

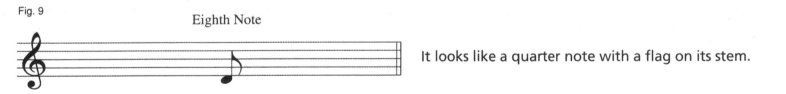

Fig. 9

Eighth Note

It looks like a quarter note with a flag on its stem.

When we divide a quarter note in half, we get two eighth notes. Thus there are eight eighth notes in a measure of 4/4 time. Each eighth note is held for half a beat.

Fig. 10

Beam

When several eighth notes are played in succession, as in Figure 10, the flags are usually replaced by *beam*s.

To feel and understand eighth notes on a rhythmic level, begin by counting slowly "**one**, two, three, four, **one**, two, three, four," etc. Next tap your foot along in steady quarter notes.

Fig. 11

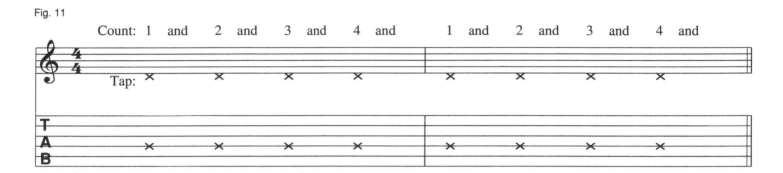

Now, *subdivide* the rhythm by counting "**ONE**-and, **two**-and, **three**-and, **four**-and," etc., evenly while continuing to tap the quarter-note pulse. As you count and tap, the numbers should coincide with the taps, and the "and"s should occur exactly halfway between numbers. Be sure to maintain a steady tempo as you practice this.

Fig. 12

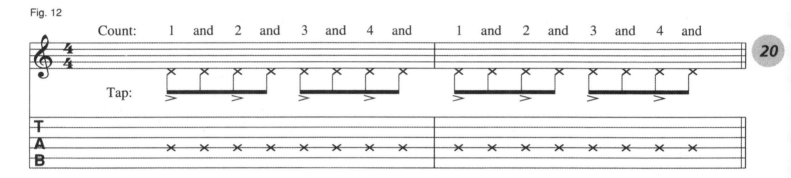

Let's apply eighth-note rhythm to the guitar. Begin by counting 4/4 time. Now, instead of tapping eighth notes, play them on the low E string, using downstrokes only.

Fig. 13

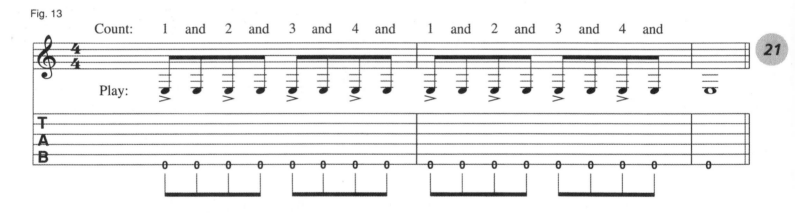

Next transfer the pattern to the open E5, A5 and D5 chords.

Fig. 14

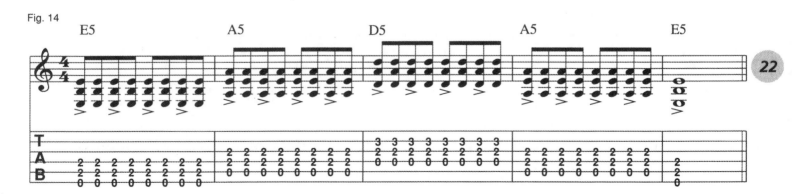

Playing Tip

When playing the following figures, take care to avoid strumming idle strings. Switching chords is a bit trickier when strumming eighth-note rhythm, so concentrate on making quick, confident changes. Slow the tempo down if necessary.

Here are some simple progressions using three-note open power chords and eighth-note rhythm in 4/4 time.

Fig. 16

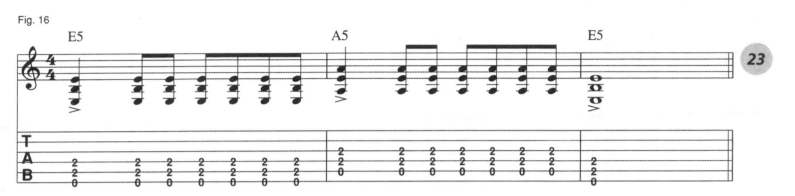

Fig. 17

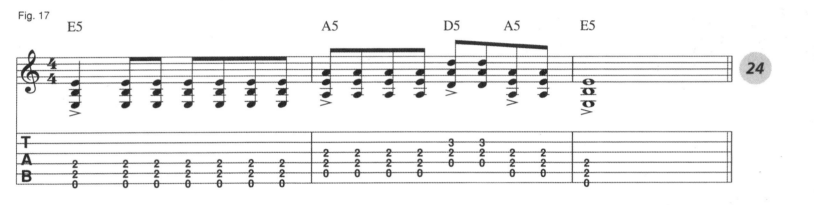

Fig. 18

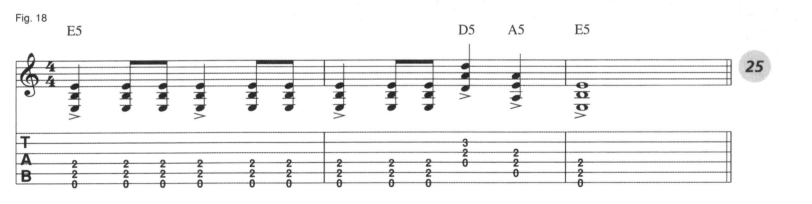

Fig. 19

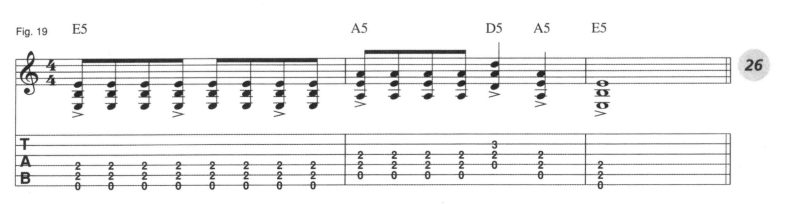

Fret-hand Muting

When playing power chords such as these, it's important that you *mute* (silence) any strings that aren't being used. This is accomplished by employing a technique known as *fret-hand muting*. Let's use the E5 chord shown below as an example:

1. Press the tip of your left index finger down on the 5th string behind the 2nd fret as before.
2. While the tip of the index finger continues to fret the fifth string, allow the side of the finger to lay lightly across the 4th-1st strings midway between the 1st and 2nd frets.
   Use just enough pressure to keep the strings from vibrating.
3. Strum the E5 chord while muting the top four strings. Even if you allow the pick to glide across all six strings, only the bottom two strings should ring.

Muted strings are indicated by X's in the tablature.

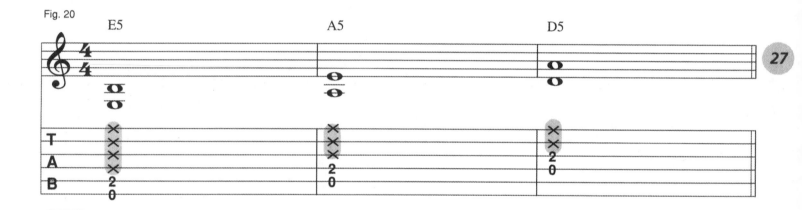

Fret-hand muting is especially important when:

1) shifting the power chord form up or down the neck

2) strumming all six strings, and

3) using distortion to fatten the tone.

All three situations are common in rock and modern guitar styles in general.

Work on switching back and forth between the following power chords and don't forget to apply fret-hand muting.

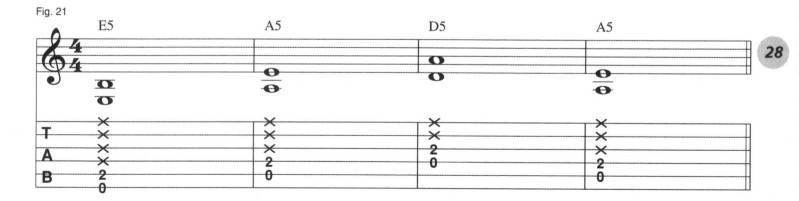

Chapter 3

SINGLE NOTE PLAYING

So far, you have been playing power chords and variations of power chords. Now, it's time to start working with single notes. Let's start playing some "riffs."

RIFFS

A *riff* is a repeated melodic figure which is structurally important in a song or solo. A riff can be thought of as a complete short musical idea. Notice that this riff uses sharps (#). A sharp (#) raises the note a half step. You play the note the next fret higher. This riff in straight quarters is an immortal rock and roll melody based on an underlying chord.

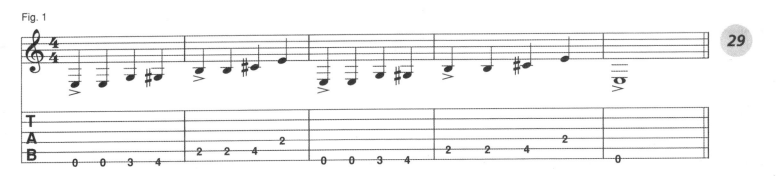

We'll build single-note riffs from chord forms. Here's an example of a simple riff in E and its related chord shape. You've heard this familiar melody in the repertoire of the Beatles, Eric Clapton and bluesmen like Freddie King and Otis Rush. Remember, practice slowly until you can play even, relaxed and accurate. Then gradually work up to faster speeds or tempos.

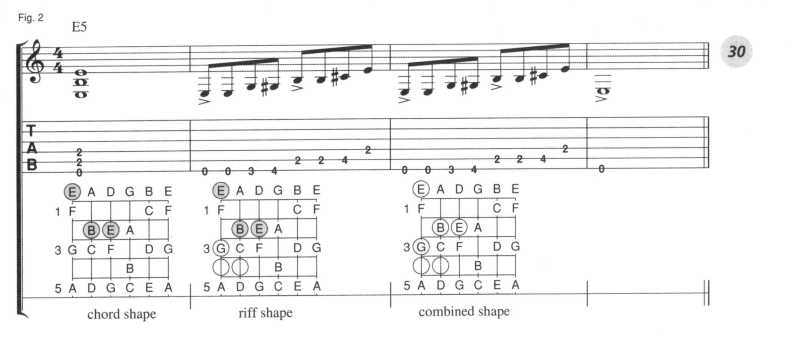

Notice that all three chord tones are included in the riff.

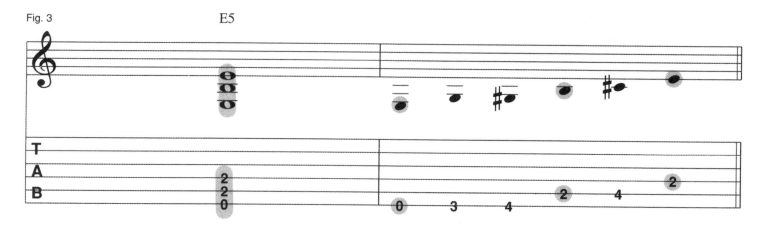

Think of chord and riff as sharing in the same positional *box*. It's a concept which launched a thousand riffs. Like a chord, a riff has a shape. Thinking of riffs this way provides you with a familiar reference point and helps you see how single note playing relates to chords.

Now let's move this riff to a different tonal center on the guitar. Here's where the chord box/melody idea really comes into play. Think of the chord and riff as a unit. Be aware of the new A root on the 5th string. Play the riff in A using the chord box and root as guiding principles.

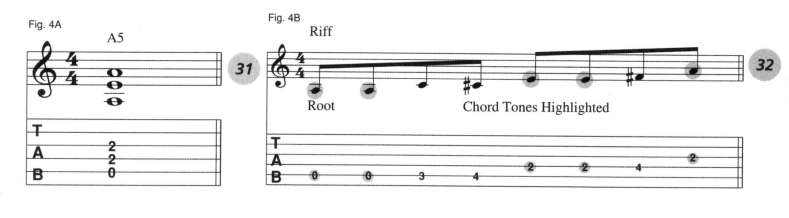

Notice the use of the *natural sign* (♮) in the second bar. A natural sign cancels any sharps or flats and returns a note to its original pitch.

Now play this riff over a D5 chord. The new root will be D on the open 4th string.

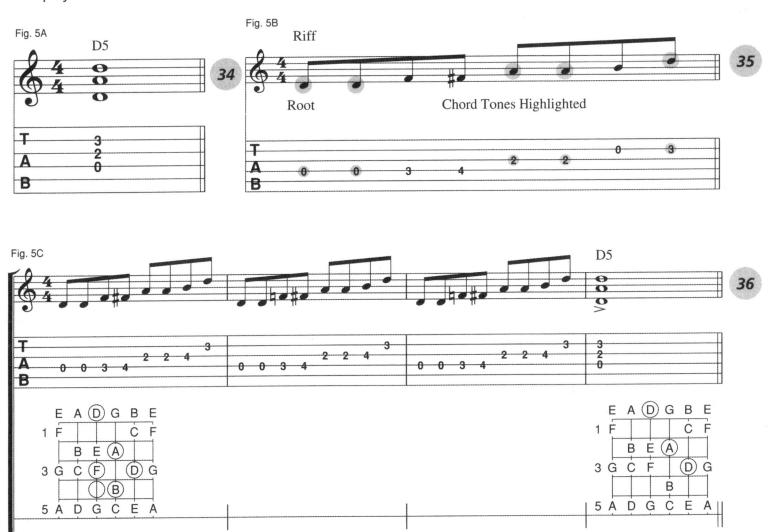

Fig. 5A

Fig. 5B
Riff
Root   Chord Tones Highlighted

Fig. 5C

For our next riff, we'll need to learn about *dotted rhythms*. A dot placed to the right of a note tells you to increase the note's duration by one half. Any type of note can be dotted — quarters, eighths, halves, wholes, etc.

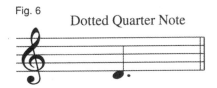

Fig. 6
Dotted Quarter Note

This is the symbol for a dotted quarter note.
It gets held for one and a half beats.

Establish the eighth-note subdivision in your ears, tap the dotted-quarter/eighth rhythm while counting even eighth notes ("**ONE**-and, **two**-and, **three**-and, **four**-and, **ONE**-and, **two**-and, **three**-and, **four**-and, **ONE**," etc.). The notes will be struck on **one**, the "**and**" of two, **three** and the "**and**" of four. Keep doing this until you feel you've got the hang of it.

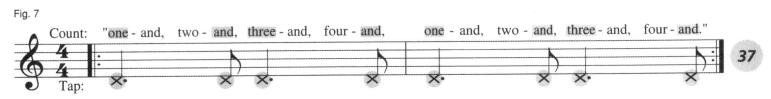

Fig. 7
Count: "one - and, two - and, three - and, four - and,   one - and, two - and, three - and, four - and."
Tap:

Notice that the two bars shown have *repeat marks* at the beginning and end. The music between repeat marks is played twice. In this example, you count out the two measures shown, and then go back and count them out again, without any break in the meter.

Now, transfer the rhythm to your instrument. Instead of tapping the dotted quarter/eighth rhythm pattern with your hand, play it on the low E string while counting eighth notes. Proceed slowly at first until you develop enough coordination to play it faster.

Fig. 8

The following riff has a classic rockabilly/early rock and roll flavor as in the music of Elvis Presley, Carl Perkins and Fats Domino. It is built around the open E5 power chord shape and employs the dotted-quarter/eighth rhythm in the first two beats.

Fig. 9

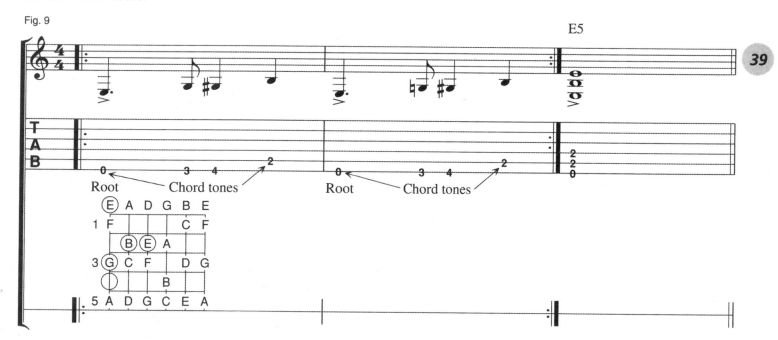

Now, transfer this riff so that you can play it over an A5 chord. The new root will now be A on the open 5th string. Here it is.

Fig. 10

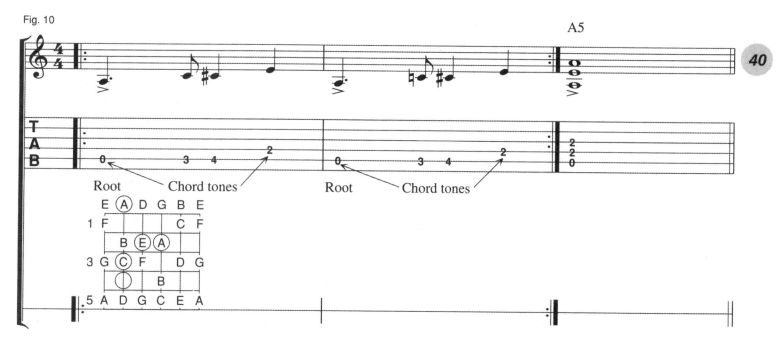

Now, transfer this riff so that you can play it over a D5 chord. The new root will now be D on the open 4th string. Here it is.

Fig. 11

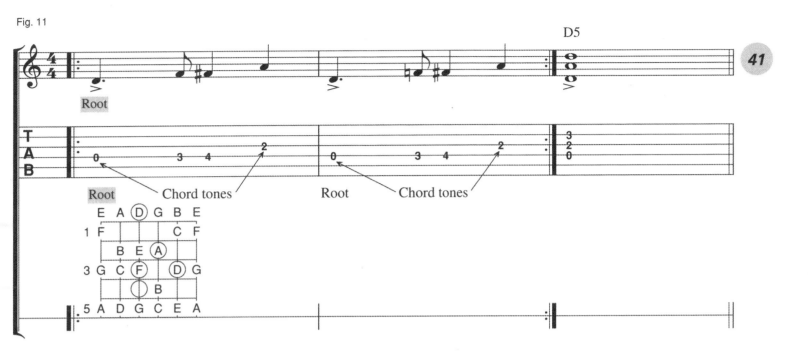

PALM MUTING

Palm muting is a technique whereby you rest the heel of your pick-hand palm on the strings as you pick.
It is important to rest directly on the bridge, not in front of it or behind it.
If you are in front of the bridge (on the side closer to the neck), you will be *over-muting* —your sound will be too muffled and your pitches may be affected
If you are behind the bridge, you will be *under-muting* —
your sound will not be muffled enough, and may not be muffled at all.
This technique imparts a percussive, muffled/chunky sound to the string's tone and is desirable as an effect in many styles of music such as rock, metal, r&b, country, pop and fusion, to name a few.

Palm muting is indicated by the abbreviation "P.M." appearing directly above the tablature.

To familiarize yourself with the palm muting technique, first play this open A note in a steady eighth-note rhythm using all downstrokes.

Fig. 12

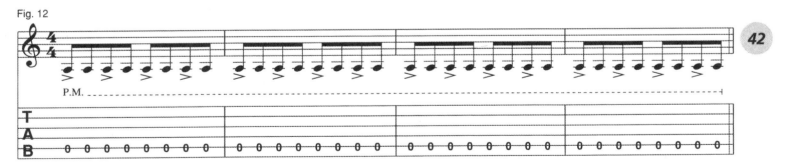

You should notice a thicker sound which is especially effective when using distortion. The muting effect can be regulated by varying the amount of pressure and hand flesh you apply to the strings.

SIXTEENTH-NOTES

Sixteenth-note rhythm is a familiar fixture in rock, metal and many other forms of music. This is the symbol for a single *16th note*.

Fig. 13

16th Note

It looks like an eighth note with two flags on its stem.

There are four 16th notes per beat. Each is held for one quarter of a beat. We are simply dividing an eighth note in half or a quarter note into four equal parts. When 16ths are played in groups, the two flags are replaced by two beams. Here's one measure of 16th notes to illustrate. Play the D note on the open fourth string.

Fig. 14

16th Notes

43

P.M.

Let's get acquainted with 16ths rhythmically. Count "**one**, two, three, four, **one**, two, three, four" slowly and evenly in 4/4 meter. Now tap quarter notes on each beat. To get the 16th-note subdivision in our ears, count "**ONE**-ee--AND-uh, **two**-ee--AND-uh, **three**-ee--AND-uh, **four**-ee--AND-uh, **ONE**-ee--AND-uh, **two**-ee--AND-uh, **three**-ee- -AND-uh, **fou**r-ee--AND-uh," etc., while continuing to tap the quarter-note pulse. Each syllable represents one 16th note.

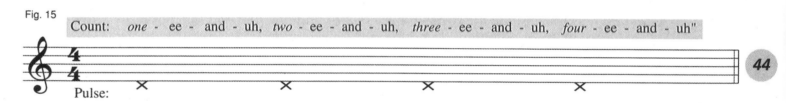

Fig. 15

Count: *one* - ee - and - uh, *two* - ee - and - uh, *three* - ee - and - uh, *four* - ee - and - uh"

Pulse:

44

ALTERNATE PICKING

To play 16th notes, we'll need to learn a new technique called *alternate picking*. Alternate picking involves alternating between downstrokes and upstrokes.

Here's the symbol for a downstroke (⊓). Pick down — glide the pick across the string(s) moving down, toward the floor.

Here's the symbol for an upstroke (∨). Pick up — Glide the pick across the string(s); moving up, away from the floor.

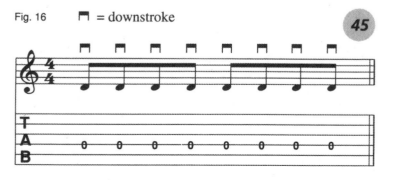

Fig. 16   ⊓ = downstroke   45

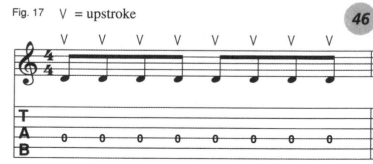

Fig. 17   ∨ = upstroke   46

Play the following using alternate picking. Try counting while playing steady 16th notes, accenting the first 16th note of each beat.

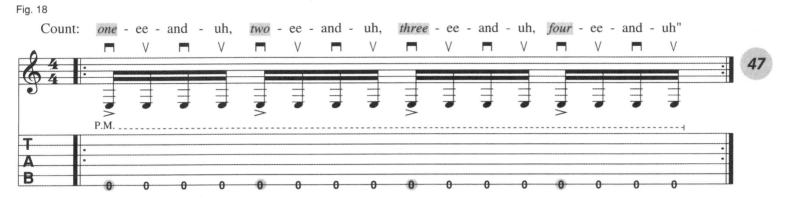

Now, let's use sixteenth notes in riffs. This one has a heavy metal quality: bands like Judas Priest, Black Sabbath and Dio as well as guitar giants such as Randy Rhoads and Yngwie Malmsteen have exploited similar figures.

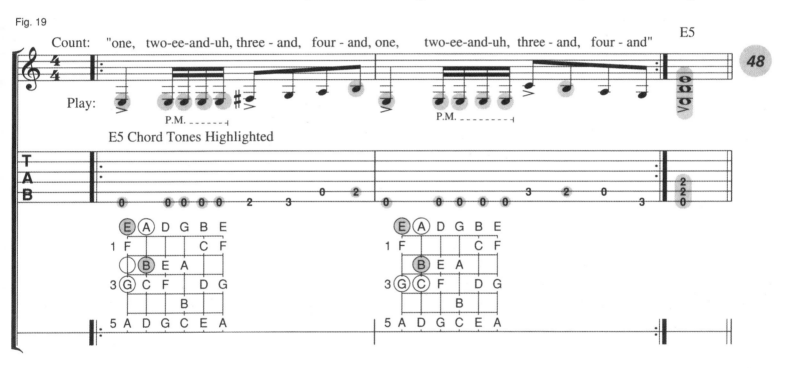

Let's play this riff over an A5 chord. Remember the root is now the open A, 5th string.

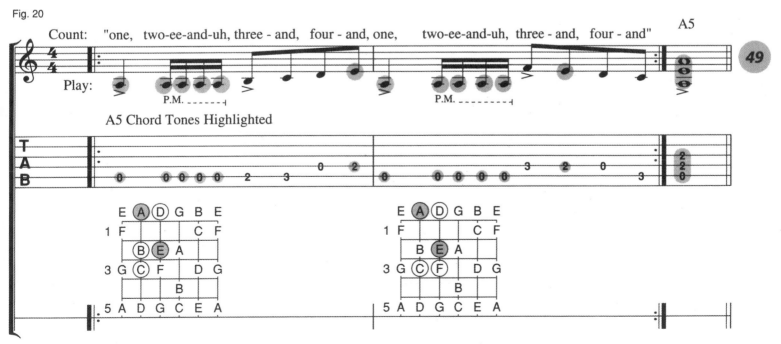

Let's subject our heavy metal riff from Figure 19 to similar movement/re-location. We'll move it to D. Play this D5 open power chord first.

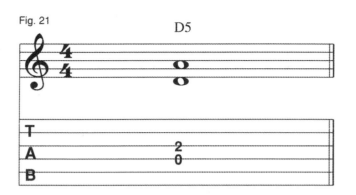

Fig. 21

Now re-locate the riff from its original E center to D. Move the E root on the 6th string to the D root on the 4th string and build the riff around the new chord shape.

In the following figure, notice the use of a flat sign (b). A flat (b) lowers the note a half step. You play the note the next fret lower.

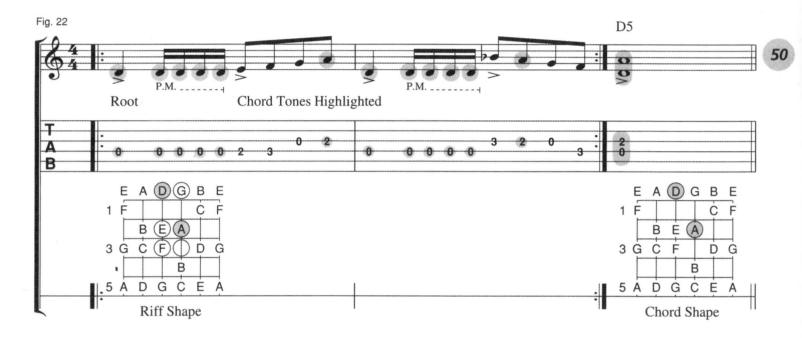

Fig. 22

The next riff is in steady eighths — a standard hard rock feel. Again, be aware of the E5 shape in the riff melody.

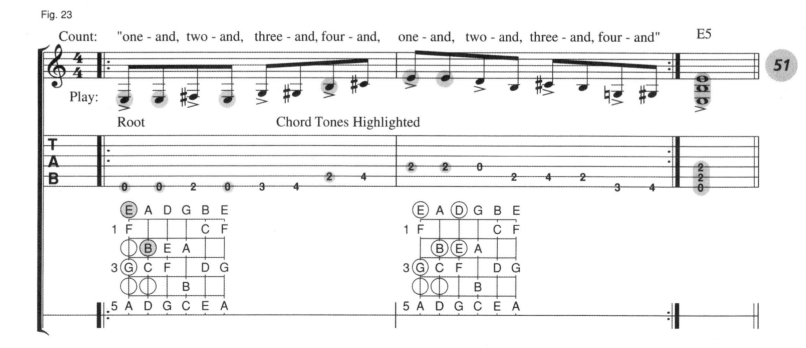

Fig. 23

30

Let's play this riff over an A5 chord. Remember the root is now the open A, 5th string.

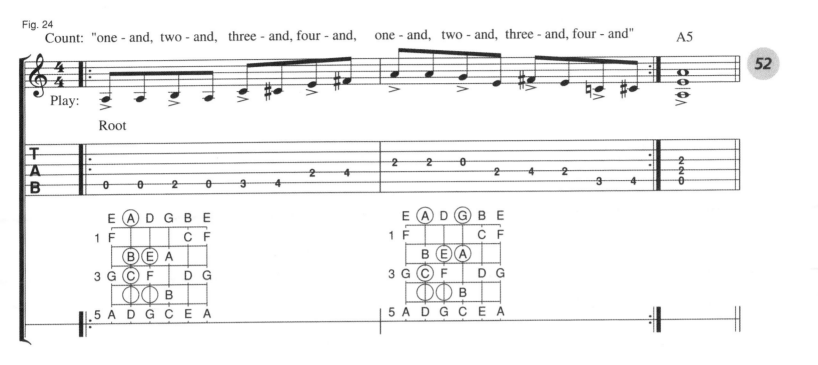

Fig. 24

Count: "one - and, two - and, three - and, four - and,   one - and, two - and, three - and, four - and"   A5

Play:

Root

Let's play this riff over a D5 chord. Remember the root is now the open D, 4th string.

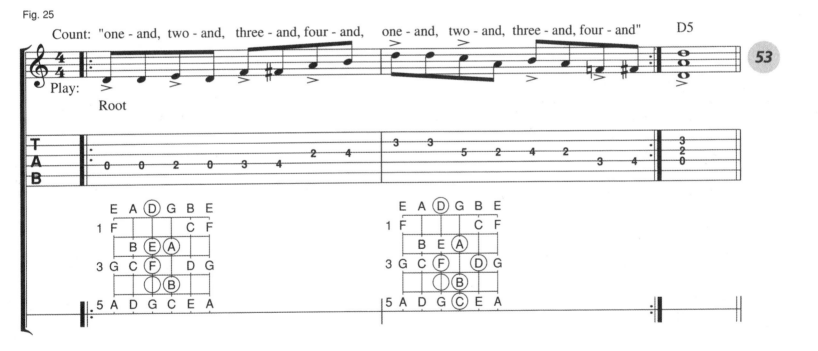

Fig. 25

Count: "one - and, two - and, three - and, four - and,   one - and, two - and, three - and, four - and"   D5

Play:

Root

MUSIC BUILDERS

As in the beginning of the book, we need to add some essentials you should know. Before you move on to the next chapter, look over the following two pages. It will help further your understanding of music basics.

POSITIONS

A *position* on the guitar is a group of four consecutive frets, one for each left-hand finger. A position is named after the lowest numbered fret in the group.

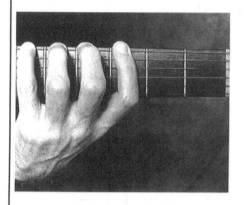
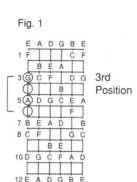

Fig. 1

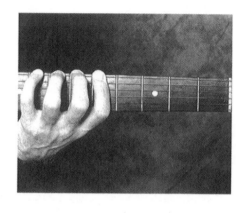

Fig. 2

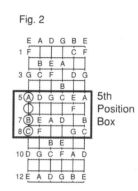

Third position - frets 3 through 6

Fifth position - frets 5 through 8

This is one of the most important concepts in single-note playing. By playing in positions, you automatically know which fingers to use.

First position is unique because, in addition to the four frets (which any position has), it also includes the open strings.

Here's an exercise to help you understand first position, and to gain strength and independence in all four left-hand fingers. Start by fretting the first string at the first fret. For now, we'll use all downstrokes.

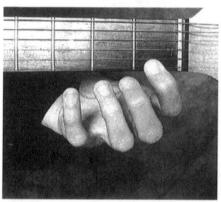

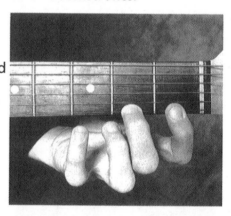

Pick the string, using a downstroke.

Now, leaving the first finger where it is, add the second finger at the second fret on the same string. Keep the fingers curved, play on the tips of the fingers, and stay close to the frets.

Pick the string, with a downstroke.

Now, leaving the first and second fingers where they are, add the third finger at the third fret.

Pick the string using a downstroke.

Finally, leaving fingers 1, 2 and 3 in place, add the fourth finger at the fourth fret.

Pick the string with a downstroke. To complete the exercise, repeat this entire sequence on each string. Be sure to leave each finger in place as you add the next finger.

Generally, lifting fingers as you move **up** a string is wasted motion. If this motion is exaggerated, it will slow you down, cause unnecessary string noise, and may tire your hand. Begin the good habit of leaving fingers in place any time you move **up** a single string.

HALF STEPS AND WHOLE STEPS

The most basic building block of music is the *half step*. It is defined as the distance from any note to the nearest next possible note. On the guitar, it is a distance of one fret.

Fig. 3

Because the guitar has more than one string, you can find half steps between notes on different strings. For example, if you play at the fourth fret on the second string, and then the open first string, you are playing a half step.

Fig. 4

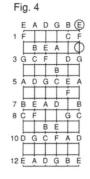

The distance of two frets, whether on one string or across two strings, is called a *whole step*. For example, if you play an open E on the first string, and then play the second fret on the first string, you are playing a whole step.

SHARPS AND FLATS

Most of the notes that you have played so far come from a group called the *natural notes*. These are the notes you get by playing the white keys on a keyboard instrument. In any octave, there are seven natural notes, and then the pattern repeats.

In between the white keys, there are five black keys. These play notes that are called *accidental* or *chromatic* notes and as we learned in this chapter are expressed as sharps and / or flats. Every accidental has two names. Let's look at this on the guitar.

Play the Eb/D# note on the open fourth string.

Fig. 5

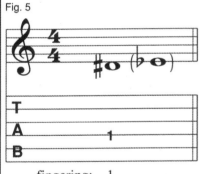

fingering: 1

You can think of this chromatic note in two ways — as a lowered E which would be called E flat and written Eb, or as a raised D, which would be called D sharp and written D#. Every chromatic can be called either a sharp or a flat. A sharp sign (#) raises the pitch of a note one half step. A flat sign (b) lowers the pitch of a note one half step. Here are all the notes on the D string from first to twelfth frets with both sets of chromatic names shown.

Fig. 6

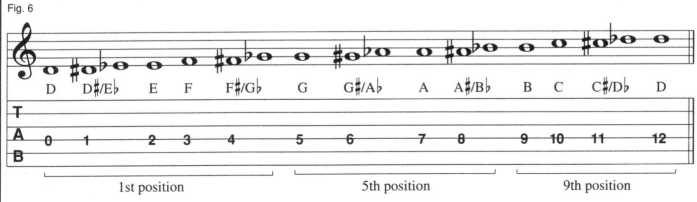

The use of a sharp as opposed to a flat depends on melodic direction and is an important part of *melodic function*.

THE 12-BAR BLUES PROGRESSION

Twelve-bar blues progressions have been found in the repertoires of the greatest rock guitarists from Hendrix to Van Halen. They are the most important progressions in blues and rock and roll. They're also encountered frequently in jazz, country and pop music.

Twelve-bar blues progressions have a very specific *form* . Form refers to the shape of a musical composition. All twelve-bar blues, for example, are divided into three *phrases*, (or musical ideas) each of which is four bars in length (3 X 4=12). (The term *bar* when used in this way is synonymous with the term *measure*.)

1st phrase: first four bars (1-4)
2nd phrase: second four bars (5-8)
3rd phrase: last four bars (9-12)

We'll play in the *key* of A to begin with. (A key is a set of notes related in a particular way to a specific note called the *tonic*. In the key of A, all the notes and chords relate back to the note A, which is the tonic in that key.)

Let's use the A5, D5 and E5 power chords that we learned earlier. These three chords will be designated by the Roman numbers I, IV and V, respectively. It is common practice to refer to chords by the number of the scale step on which the root of the chord falls. Thus:

Scale Step	1	2	3	4	5	6	7	8(1)
Note Name	A	B	C	D	E	F	G	A
Chord Numeral	I			IV	V			

This is a very important concept.

The chords fit into the phrases as follows:
I (A5) for the first four bars;

IV to I (D5 to A5) for the next four bars;

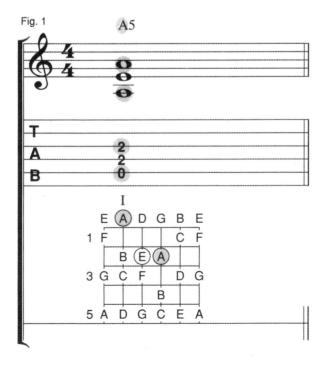

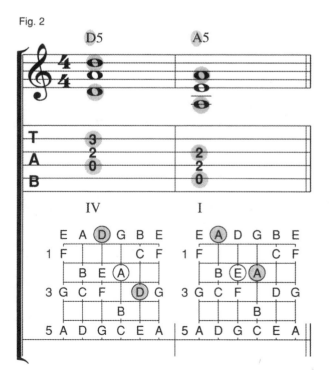

and V to IV to I (E5 to D5 to A5) in the final four bars.

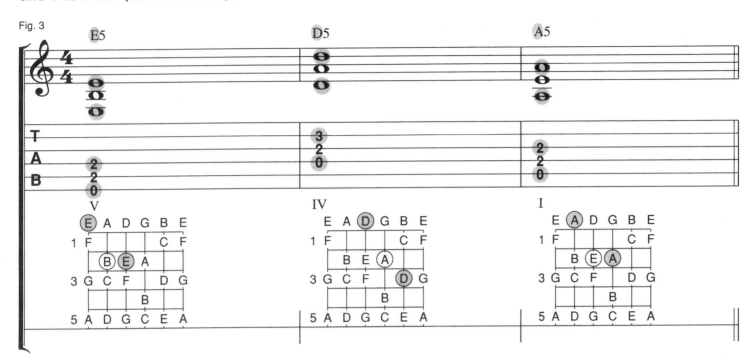

Play each of these phrases now, separately. We'll give them a simple whole-note rhythm (one strum per bar).

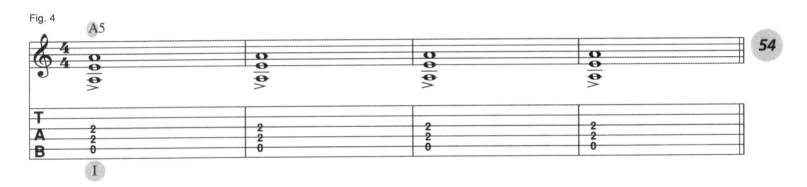

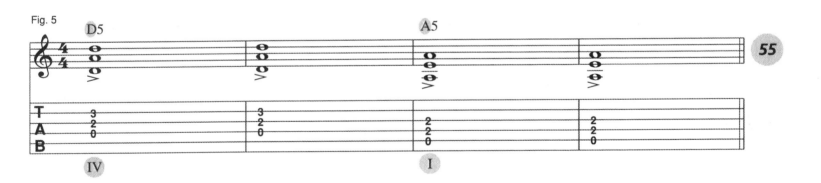

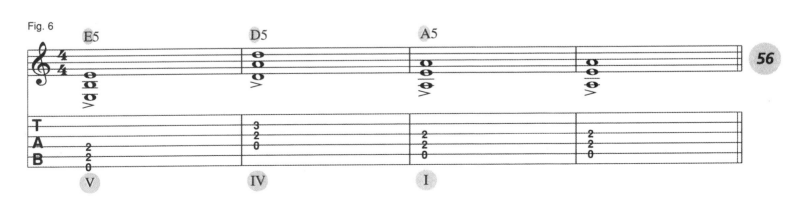

Learning sections of a song before trying to master the entire song is always the best way to practice.

Now let's play the entire 12-bar progression in whole-note rhythm.

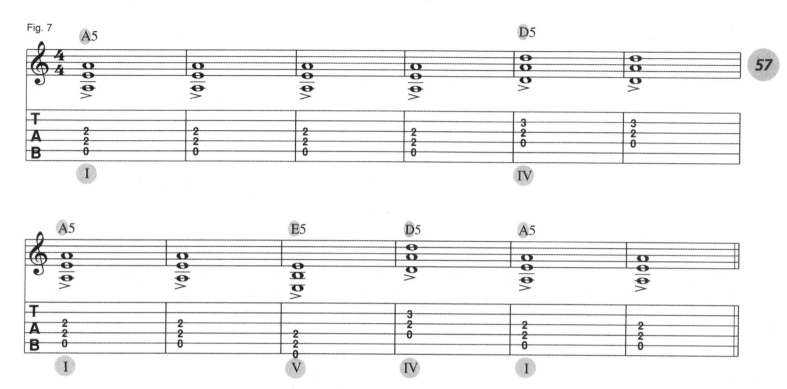

Here's the same progression with quarter-note rhythms (four strums per bar).

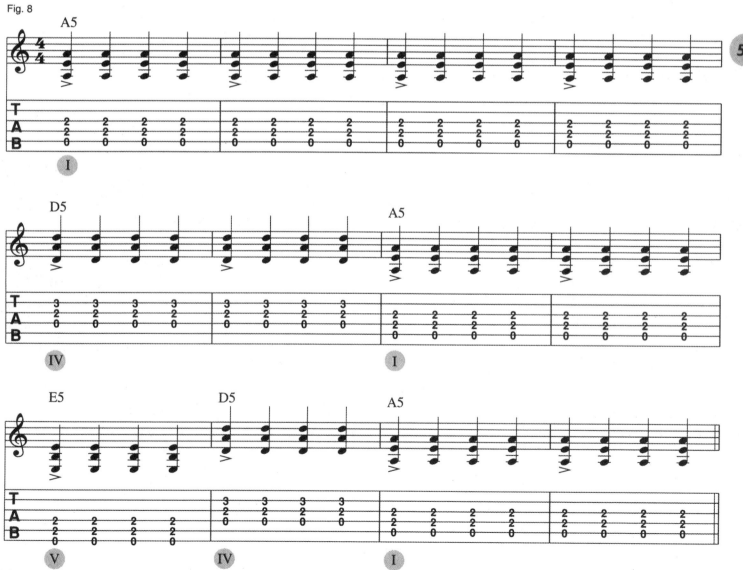

BLUES COMPING

Our next step will be to learn and add the two-note *sixth chord* to the changes and create a simple, but absolutely essential, *comping* (accompaniment) figure. We'll combine the sixth chord in patterns with the root-fifth power chord shapes we already know. This is the simplest type of *chord extension* possible. Chord extension is the process whereby notes are added to a chord and the altered chord is used in place of the original chord in a progression.

Recall that the open A5 power chord is built on the interval structure of root and fifth (A + E). A sixth chord, for our purposes, is built on the interval structure of root and sixth (A + F#).

1	2	3	4	5	6	7	8(1)
A	B	C	D	E	F#	G	A
1(A)		+			6(F#) equals A6		
root					sixth		

Here are the A5 and A6 forms side by side. Play them now. You've heard countless variations of this pattern in the music of Chuck Berry, the Stones, Aerosmith, Kiss, Van Halen and Guns 'N' Roses.

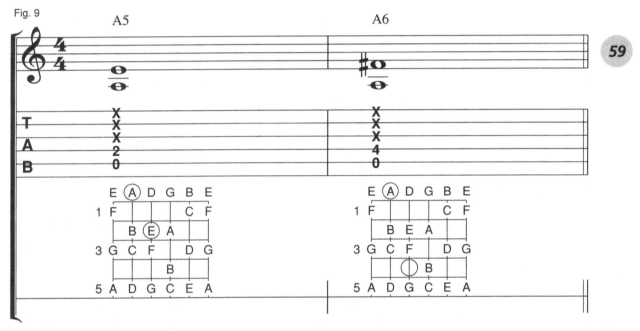

Fig. 9

59

Notice how closely related the two chords are.

The E in the A5 chord moves up to F# in the sixth chord. The root (A) remains constant.

Practice alternating between the two chords now. Keep the E fretted with the index finger as you fret the F# with the ring finger.

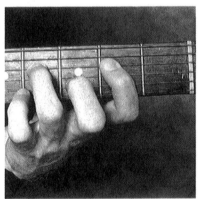

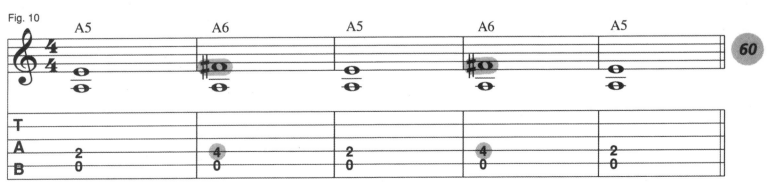

Fig. 10

60

Let's play these shapes in rhythm. Play the following pattern in quarter notes, changing chords on every beat.

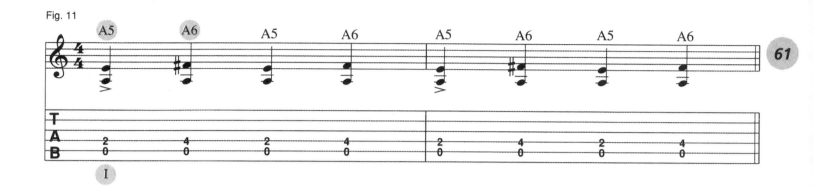

Notice the sense of motion created by alternating between the fifth and sixth. This will be the I-chord *figure* which we'll later apply to the first phrase of the 12-bar blues progression. A figure is generally several notes or chords occurring over one original chord. For example, A5 to A6 occurs over the A5 chord, in a sense replacing it.

Now let's move the fifth-sixth comp pattern over to the 4th and 3rd strings for the IV chord figure: D5 to D6. Again, it's in straight quarter-note rhythm.

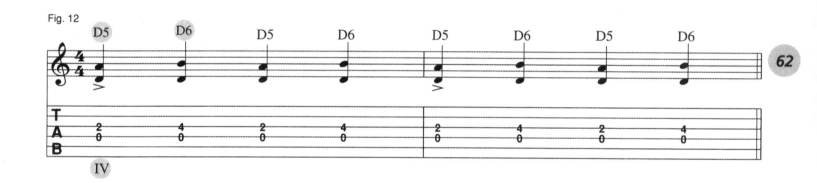

Next move the pattern over to the 6th and 5th strings for the V chord figure: E5 to E6.

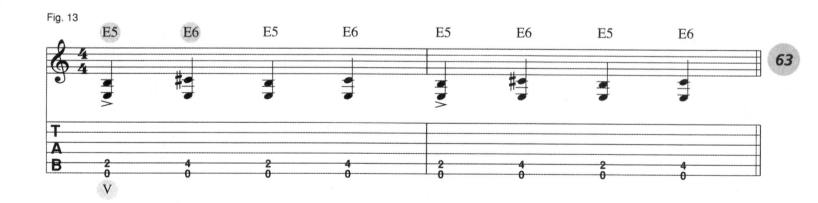

Let's put all three phrases together and play an entire 12-bar blues progression in A using the 5th-6th comp figures in place of the power chords we played earlier.

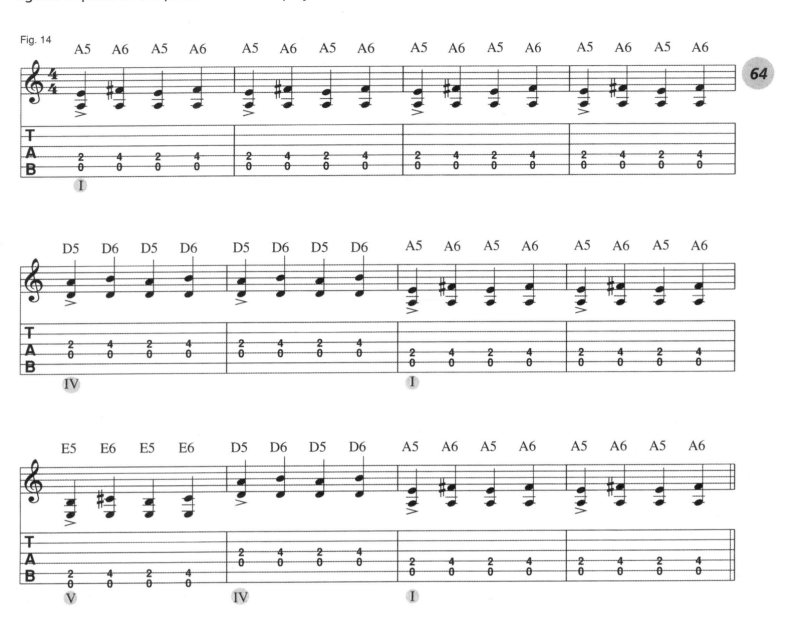

THE SHUFFLE FEEL

The *shuffle* feel is the rhythmic heartbeat of countless classic rock, blues and r&b tunes. Let's learn this all-important groove now and apply it to our fifth-sixth comp figure and to the 12-bar blues progression.

Begin by thinking of the basic eighth-note rhythm. Play this pattern: A5 to A6 in eighth notes, changing chords on every beat (on "**one**, two, three, four").

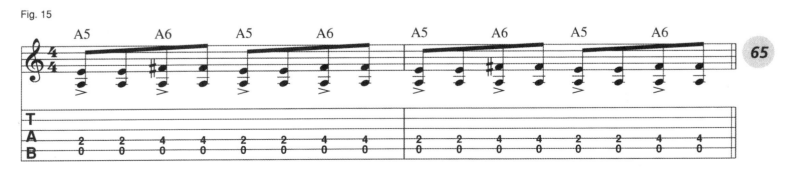

Remember to count and externalize the eighth-note rhythm first before playing the figure on the guitar.

You'll notice that this pattern relies on a regular even-eighth-note rhythm. Let's learn how to make it *swing*.

First, divide each beat into three even subdivisions. This will form an eighth-note *triplet* on each beat. Here is the symbol for an eighth-note triplet.

Fig. 16

Eighth-Note Triplet

Count and tap "**ONE**-and-uh, **two**-and-uh, **three**-and-uh, **four**-and-uh, **ONE**-and-uh, **two**-and-uh, **three**-and-uh, **four**-and-uh," etc. This syllabic representation helps you hear the triplet subdivision.

Once you feel comfortable counting and tapping triplets, play them on the guitar using three even downstroke strums. Remember to accent the downbeats.

Fig. 17

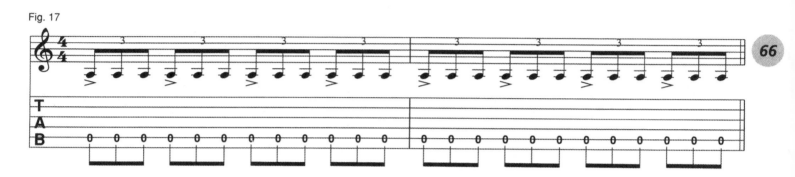

Subdividing a measure of 4/4 into triplets generates 12 eighth notes per measure. Triplets are often written in *12/8 meter* without the number three over each triplet.

Fig. 18

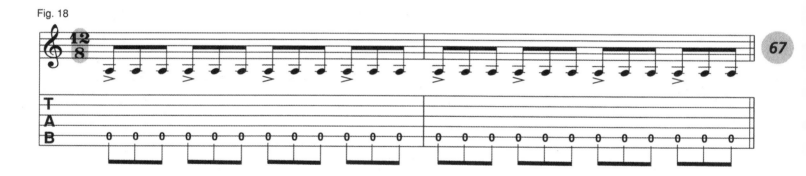

The shuffle rhythm is created by playing only the first and last eighth note of each triplet. The second eighth note is *tied* to the first. When two notes are tied, you play only the first, but you let it ring for the combined duration of the two. In this case, you play the first eighth-note, and let it ring for the same amount of time as two eighth notes.

Fig. 19A

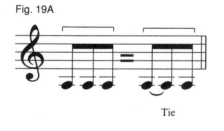

Tie

This figure is notated more simply as a quarter note followed by an eighth note.

Fig. 20

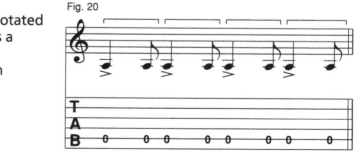

Fig. 19B

Play the following blues riff as an example. Figures like this are found in the Chicago blues styles of Muddy Waters, Otis Rush and Howlin' Wolf as well as latter day blues/rock bands like the Yardbirds, Cream and Led Zeppelin.

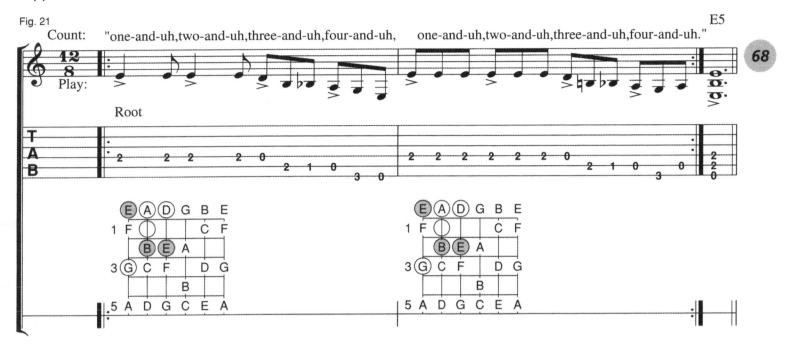

Let's play this riff over an A5 chord. Remember the root is now the open A, 5th string.

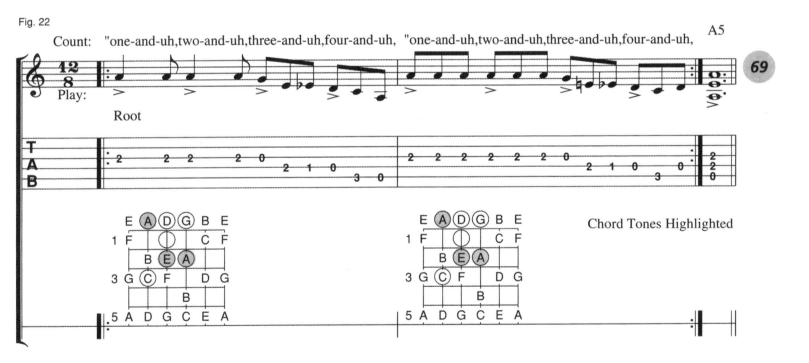

Let's play this riff over a D5 chord. The root is now the open D, 4th string.

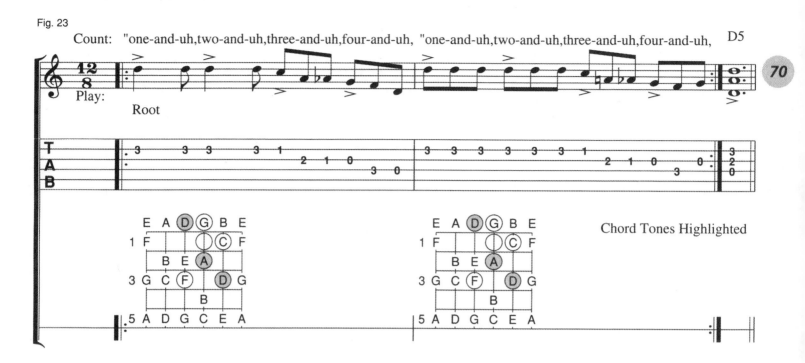

Fig. 23

Chord Tones Highlighted

Blues, metal and classical pieces are often conceived in this time signature. Play the following triplet pattern using the A5 and A6 chords to really feel the triplet groove in 12/8. Again, change chords on each downbeat. You'll strum three strokes per beat.

Fig. 24

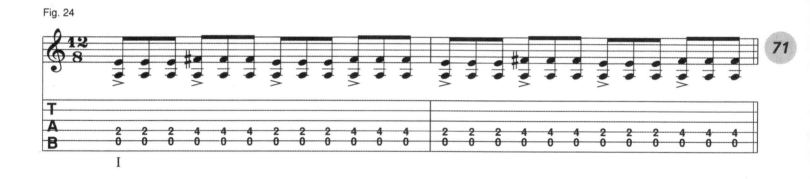

Now, back to the quarter/eighth unit. This is the nucleus of the shuffle groove. Play it now using the A5 and A6 chords. Remember, you're changing chords on each downbeat as you did with even eighth notes in 4/4, only now you're using the quarter/eighth shuffle pulse. Start moderately and keep a consistent tempo.

Fig. 25

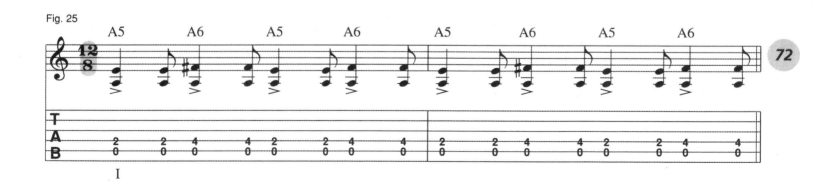

This groove is perceived and performed as a shuffle, but is often written as straight eighths in 4/4 meter for simplicity. (You will hear this called many things: *triplet feel, shuffle rhythm, swing* or *jazz eighth-notes*.) Play it now.

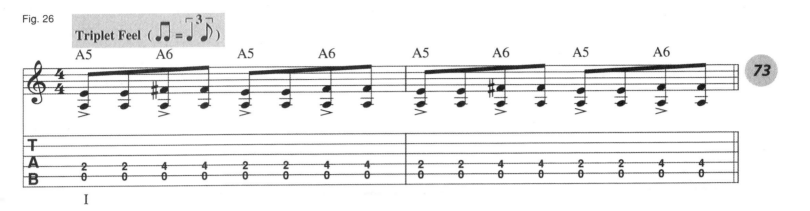

Realize that Figures 25 and 26 are the same groove notated two different ways. This immortal shuffle pattern is a familiar fixture in rock, R & B and blues rhythm guitar playing — check out Stevie Ray Vaughan's "Look At Little Sister", Chuck Berry's "Johnny B. Goode", B.T. O.'s "Takin' Care Of Business", The Allman Brothers' "Statesboro Blues" or the Beatles' "Get Back". Now let's build a simple 12-bar blues progression in A. This will employ a shuffle groove, but we'll use the triplet feel idea, keeping it in 4/4 meter. You'll be playing two-note open power chords throughout. As you recall, the first phrase is comprised of the I chord (A). Play it using the fifth-to-sixth comping figure with the shuffle rhythm.

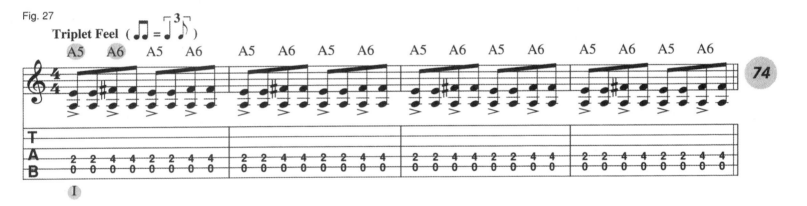

The second phrase begins on the IV chord (D) and moves back to the I chord (A) halfway through. Play this phrase and apply the shuffle groove to the changes.

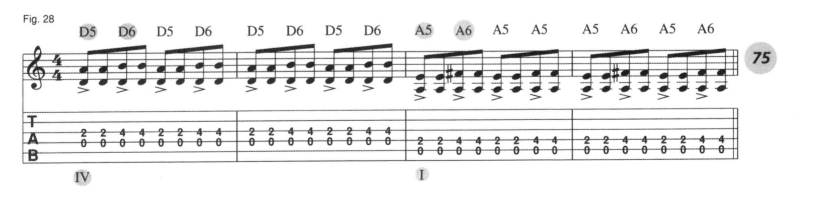

The third and final phrase begins on the V chord (E), moves to the IV chord (D) then back to the I chord (A). Play the phrase and keep it shuffling smoothly. The change from E to D is a bit tricky due to the string skip, so concentrate on this particular maneuver. Use your fret-hand thumb to help mute the lower strings as you switch.

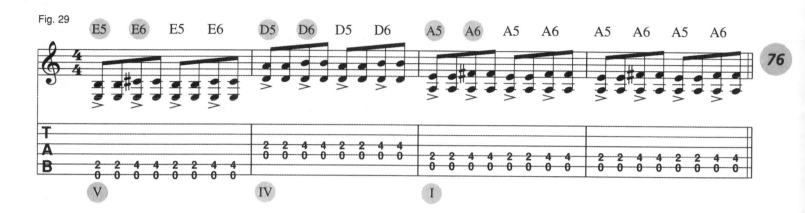

Now let's put the three phrases together to form a 12-bar blues progression in A. This is a staple in rock and modern blues style and is found in the repertoire of countless artists: ZZ Top, Van Halen, AC/DC, Led Zeppelin, as well as a host of Chicago blues guitarists. Remember, it's still a shuffle rhythm, so maintain that triplet feel.

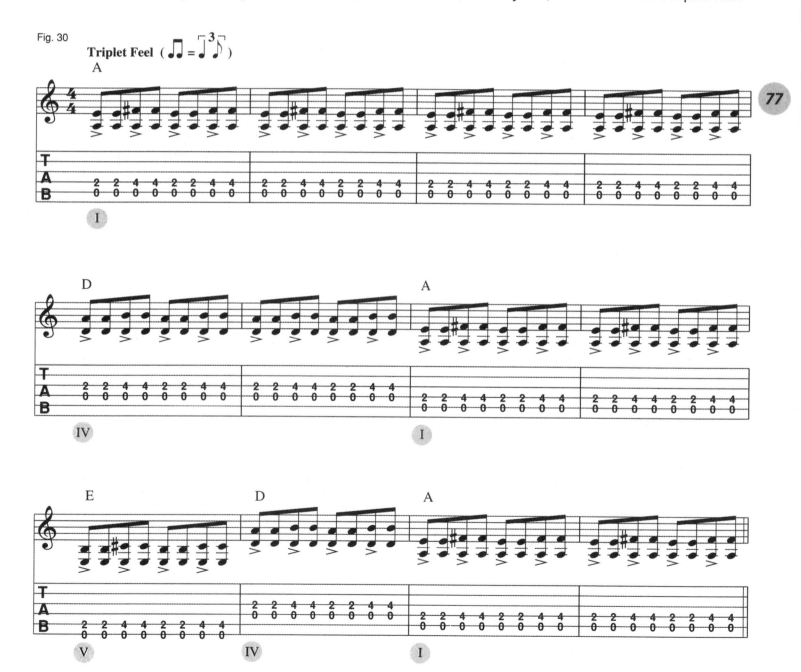

Let's expand the basic comping figure with another extension. Here's a new two-note chord, A7.

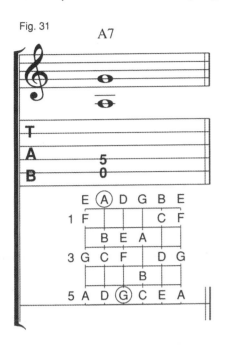

Fig. 31

This is the *seventh-chord* voicing which belongs to the same family of shapes as the open power chords you already know, like A5 (shown above) and A6. It is comprised of the root and seventh tones in its interval structure: A+G (1+7). Fret this chord with the ring finger.

1	2	3	4	5	6	**7**	8(1)
A	B	C	D	E	F	**G**	A
1(A)					+	**7(G) equals A7**	
root						**seventh**	

Let's incorporate this shape into the shuffle comping figure we just learned. Play it as the third chord of the pattern establishing this chord progression: A5-A6-A7-A6.

Fig. 32

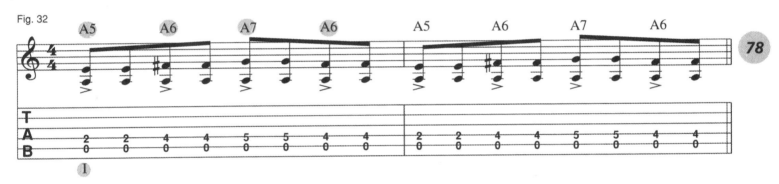

78

Listen and realize that all three chords in a blues progression function as dominant-type seventh chords . In any blues progression they are I7, IV7 and V7; in a blues progression in the key of A they are A7, D7 and E7. When you play power chords in a blues progression, you are substituting them for the seventh chords. When you use a figure such as the 5th-6th-7th figure you are also substituting the figure for the seventh chords.
Now let's apply the same shape to D and E. D7 and E7 are the result. Notice what string groups they're on.

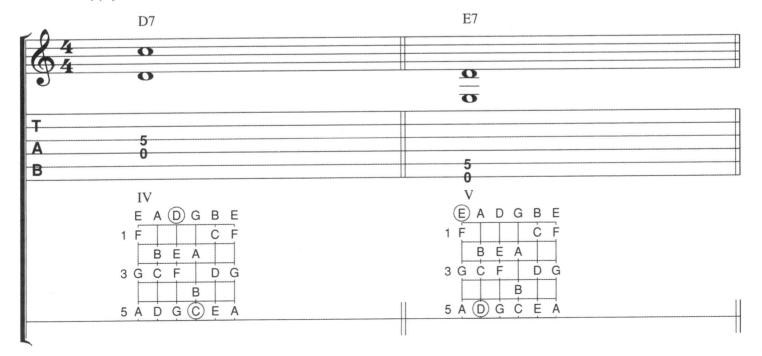

Here are two one-bar comping phrases representing the V and the IV chords in the 12-bar blues progression. The chords are E5-E6-E7-E6 for the V chord and D5-D6-D7-D6 for the IV chord. Practice them separately first, then together in time.

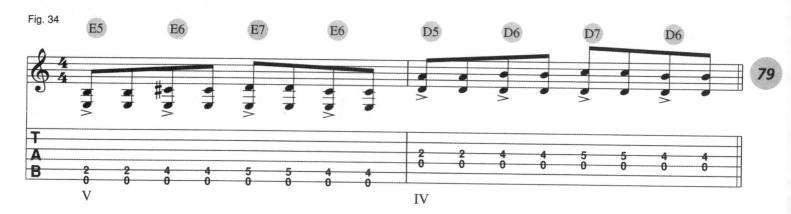

Fig. 34

Now you have all the moves under your fingers. Let's play the entire 12-bar progression using this new comping rhythm pattern of 5th-6th-7th-6th on every chord. This will again be a 12-bar in A with a shuffle groove in the style of Johnny Winter, Eric Clapton, Stevie Ray Vaughan or Chuck Berry.

Fig. 35

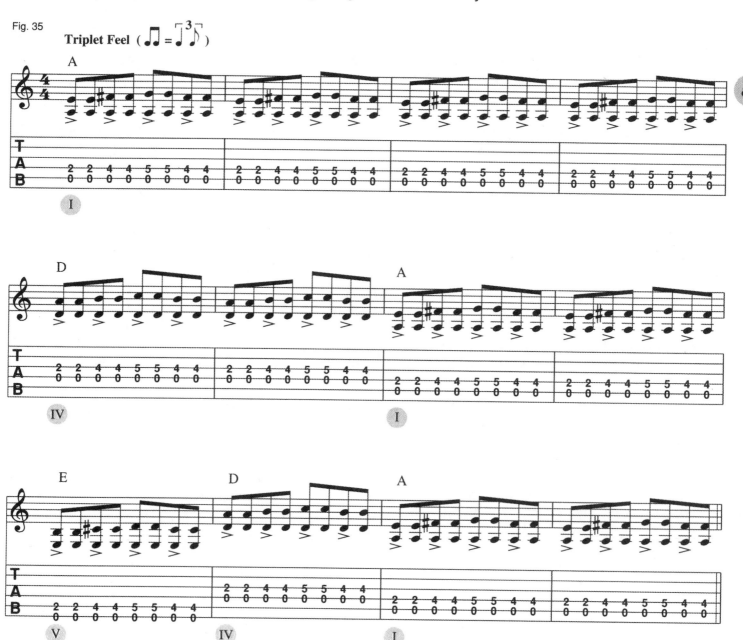

Note that in this example, the A5-A6-A7 chord changes are a figure simplified to just A. All three function, in essence, as an A chord, regardless of individual names. The same is true for the D and E chords in the progression.

MORE SINGLE NOTE PLAYING

Many riffs played in songs are taken through chord progressions. For instance, if the chords in a song are A, D and E, then the riff can be played on each of these three roots. You've heard this idea used in classic rock tunes like "Day Tripper," (the Beatles) "Welcome To The Jungle," (Guns 'N' Roses) "Sunshine Of Your Love," (Cream) "Heartbreaker," (Led Zeppelin) and "Message In A Bottle" (the Police).

Being aware of where the root is in the riff and the chord shape/melody connection simplifies the creation of movable riffs. Let's create a master riff and take it through a 12-bar blues in A to illustrate. Begin by playing this A5 open power chord to establish the I chord.

Now play this A master riff (Fig. 2) while keeping the A5 shape in mind. It has a familiar straightahead rock and roll sound reminiscent of Little Richard, the Beatles and countless other greats.

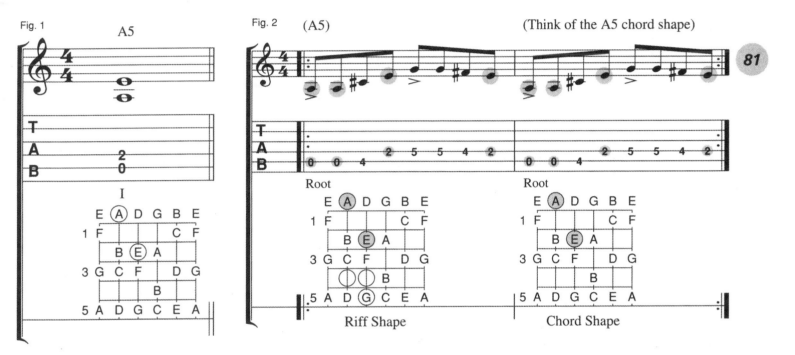

It's a one-bar melodic pattern. Remember to visualize the A5 chord shape and locate the root A on the 5th string.

Let's move the riff to the IV and V chords of the progression (D and E, respectively). Here are the shapes.

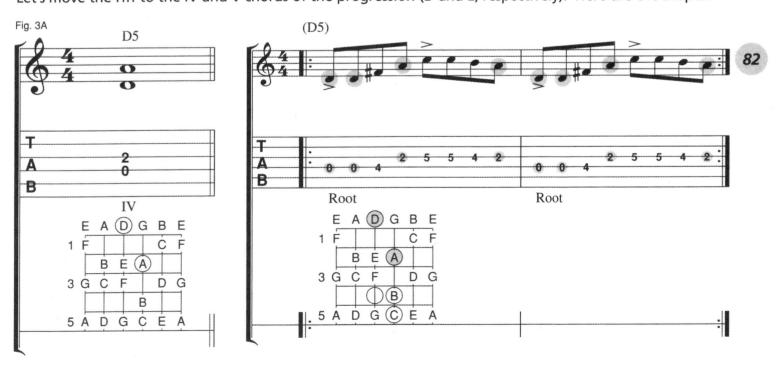

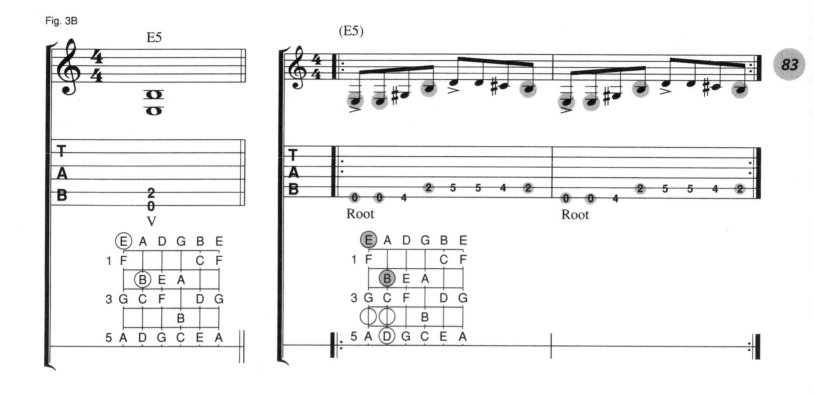

Fig. 3B

The roots D and E are on the 4th and 6th strings and the chords are D5 and E5.

Now let's apply the riff pattern to a 12-bar blues progression in A. Recall that the blues progression is comprised of three four-bar phrases. Here's the first phrase.

Fig. 4

This is the second phrase.

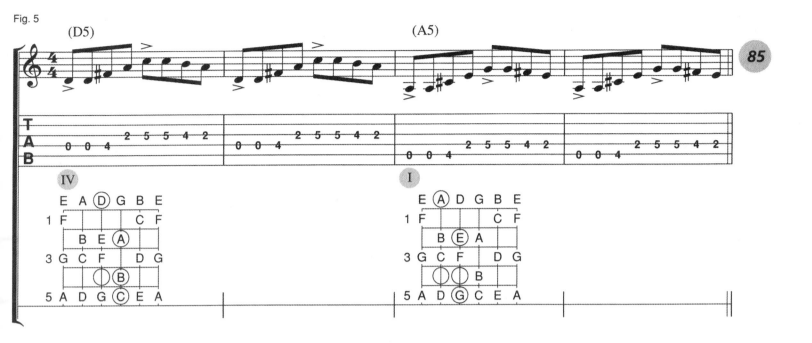

Here's the final phrase.

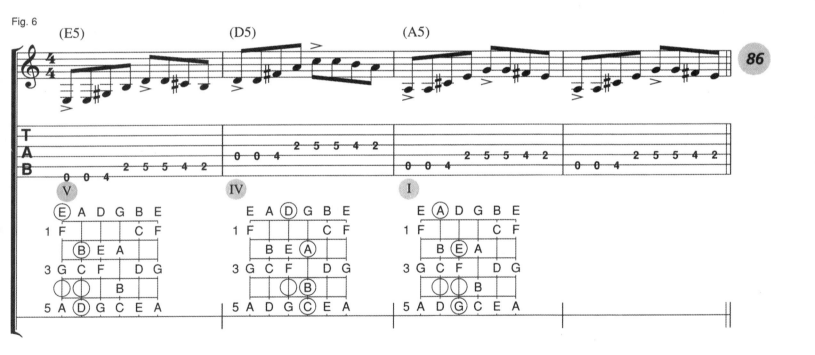

Now let's put the three phrases together to form the complete 12-bar progression. This riff-based blues pattern is prevalent in rock and blues — Little Richard's "Lucille" or the Beatles' "Birthday" are two obvious examples.

Fig. 7

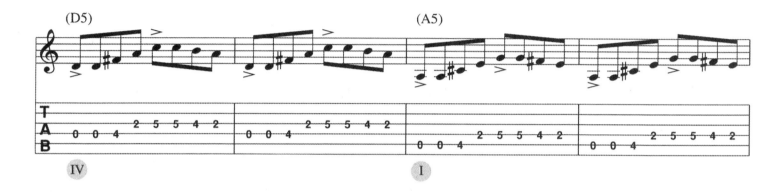

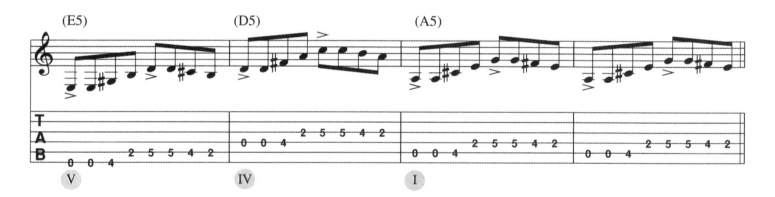

You can clearly hear how the riff melodically outlines the chordal structure of the progression.

Now let's explore a different feel with the same idea. Here's the same master riff in A with a shuffle feel. Let's play it four times to establish the pattern.

Fig. 8

Now play the entire 12-bar progression with a shuffle feel. This gives it a groove like Jeff Beck's "Rock My Plimsoul."

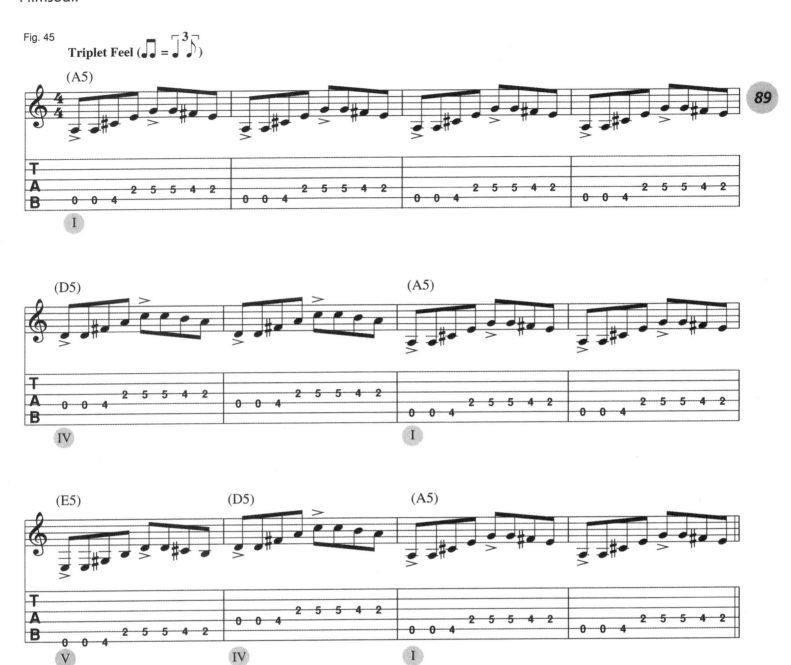

Fig. 45

Chapter 6

MINOR SOUNDS

Play the open Em chord in whole-note rhythm and let it ring for a big, spacious effect. Listen to its minor quality.

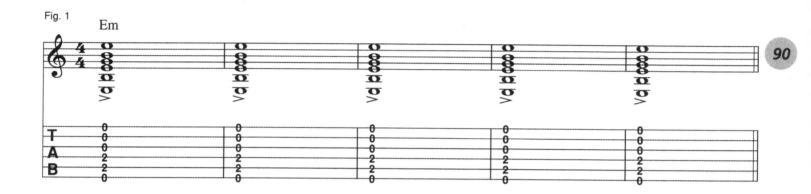

Fig. 1

90

Now strum it in steady eighth-notes.

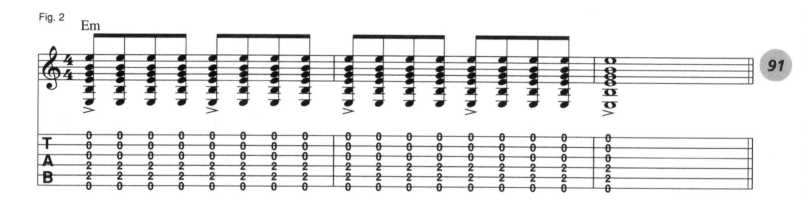

Fig. 2

91

Here's a typical rock pattern employing both Em and E5 chords. Figures like this have been employed by countless rock performers including Billy Idol, the Cars and the Police. This example combines quarter-notes and eighth-notes.

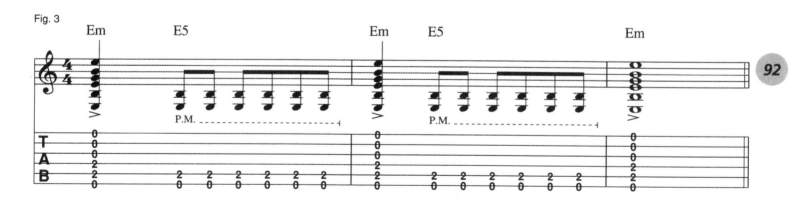

Fig. 3

92

THE MINOR-PENTATONIC SCALE

This is an E minor-pentatonic scale. It's our first official scale.

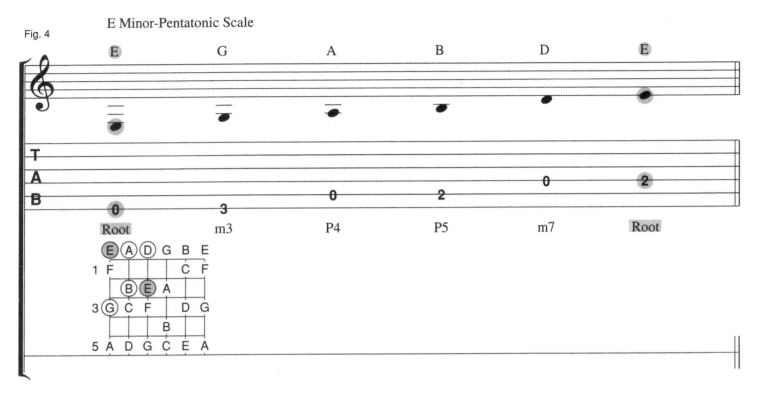

The scale is called pentatonic because it contains five notes (E,G,A,B, and D). "Penta" means five — as in pentagon or pentagram — and "tonic" means tones or notes.

Play this E minor-pentatonic scale pattern in the open position. Don't worry about rhythm for now; just practice fretting the notes on all the strings. You are in first position, so finger numbers equal fret numbers. In other words, use first finger at first fret, second finger at second fret, third finger at third fret and fourth finger at fourth fret. Notice that this entire scale is played using only second and third fingers (and open strings).

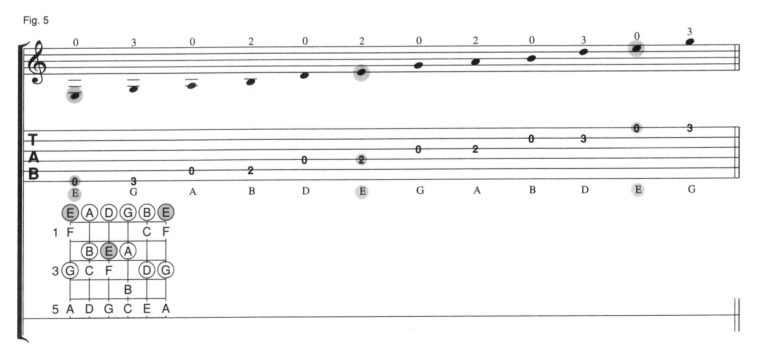

Notice the alternating pattern of open-string note, fretted note, open-string note, fretted note, etc.

We have just opened the door to open-string lead playing — so indispensible in blues, rock and country styles, as exemplified by such guitarists as Jimi Hendrix, Stevie Ray Vaughan, Joe Perry, Jimmy Page and countless others. You've heard it before — it's a familiar part of the rock guitar vocabulary. Just check out Jimi's "Voodoo Chile (Slight Return)" or Stevie Ray's "Pride And Joy."

Using a steady quarter-note rhythm, play the pattern in ascending form, beginning on the open 6th string (E) and proceeding up to the 1st string / 3rd fret (G).

Now play the same pattern in descending order, beginning on the 1st string / 3rd fret and ending on the open 6th string.

Let's combine the ascending and descending patterns into one continuous line using eighth-note rhythm. Use alternate picking.

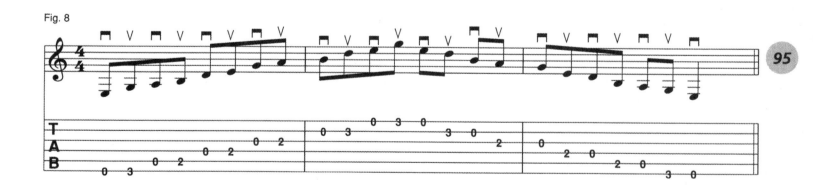

When alternate picking is used on eighth-note figures, play downstrokes on the numbers and upstrokes on the "ands". This is done regardless of which string was last attacked (if there is a string change involved) or which direction your previous pick stroke may have been. Pick direction in strict alternate picking is tied to counting, not to your last motion.

Notice that all the notes of the open Em chord are included in the E minor-pentatonic scale pattern. Here's a visual representation showing the common tones.

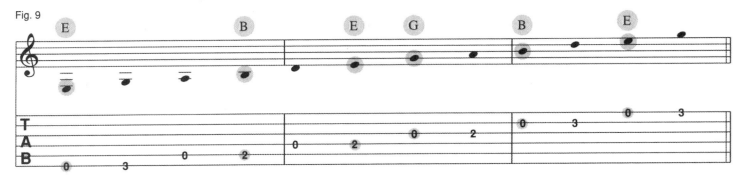

Fig. 9

Em Chord Tones Highlighted

E **G** A **B** D **E** = E minor-pentatonic scale

E **G** **B** **E** = E minor chord

Be aware of this minor chord shape as it exists inside the minor-pentatonic scale pattern. This creates its "box" identity. The following exercise integrates the Em chord with the E minor-pentatonic scale to develop the ear, hand and mind. Play the scale, pausing on each chord tone, then play the chord to reinforce the harmonic relationship.

Fig. 10

96

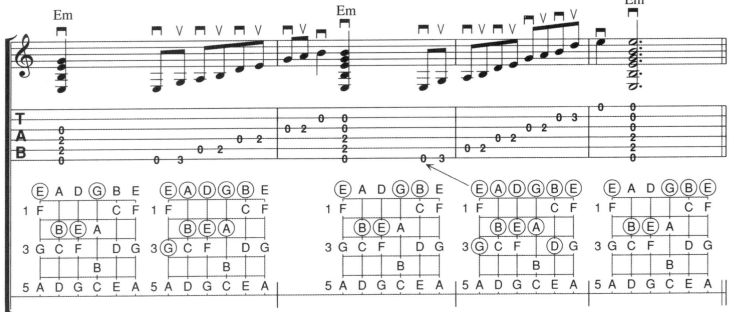

Now let's create a *motif* using notes from the E minor-pentatonic scale. A motif is a relatively short melodic / rhythmic idea. You can think of it as a short riff even though it doesn't have to recur in the same way musically. Let's examine how a motif can be developed for soloing. Play this five-note motif on the top three strings. Note the use of eighth-note rhythm and the change in direction (ascending to descending). Use alternate picking.

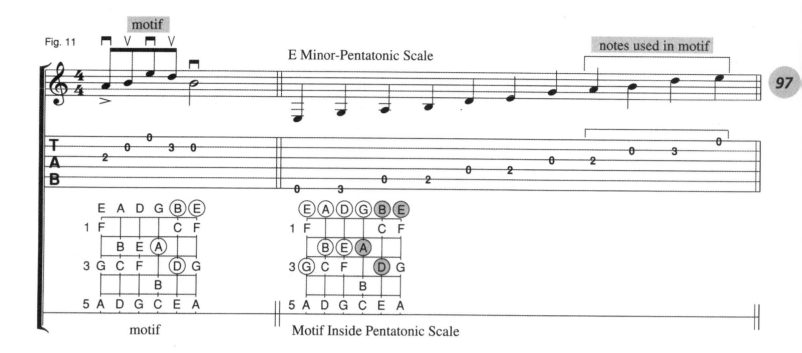

The simplest form of *motific development* is *repetition*. Let's play the motif twice to experience repetition at this basic level.

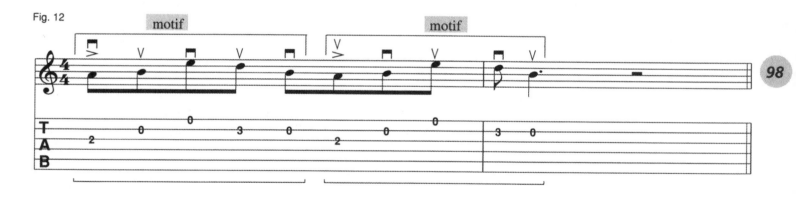

Play the motif three more times to reinforce the idea.

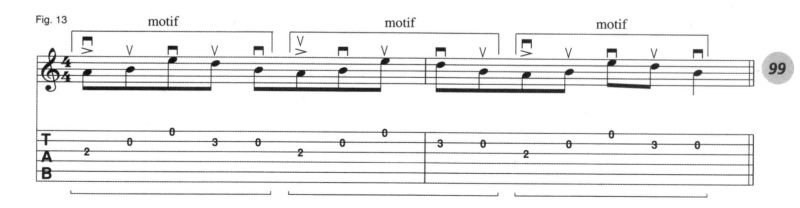

If you were to continue repeating the motif, you'd create an *ostinato* figure. (Ostinato is defined as a short musical figure that repeats persistently.) Ostinato riffs are can be found in many styles of music, including blues, rock, metal, country and jazz and are essential tools in the lead guitar approach of Michael Schenker, Stevie Ray Vaughan, Jimmy Page and Angus Young.

Notice in the previous example how the motif becomes *rhythmically displaced* with each repeat — that is, the first note of the motif no longer coincides with a beat. This type of displacement occurs whenever you repeat an odd number of notes (five in this case) while using an even subdivision such as eighth notes. Many players use this as a technique to good musical effect. It is a strong rhythmic tool in soloing.

Play the five-note motif repeatedly in eighth-note rhythm to create a displaced ostinato figure. Be careful to use correct alternate picking. Many players such as Jeff Beck, John McLaughlin and Eric Johnson use this as a technique to good musical effect.

CD Players: For tracks 100-113, start at Track 99 and use your CD *scan* function. Each track is announced.

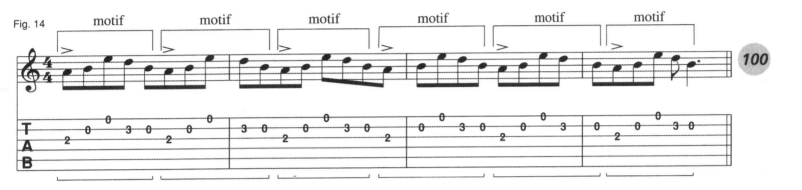

Fig. 14

100

MUSIC BUILDERS

As in the beginning of the book, we need to add some essentials you should know. Before you move on to the next chapter, look over the following three pages. It will help further your understanding of music basics.

This is an open *E minor chord* (Em). Notice that it includes the shape of the E5 power chord within its six-note voicing.

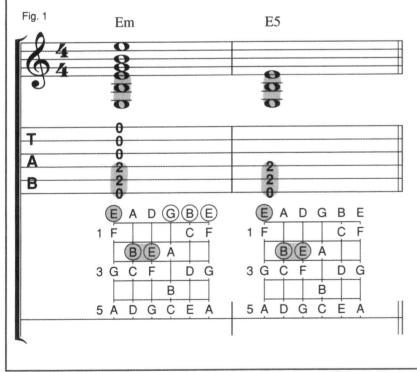

Fig. 1

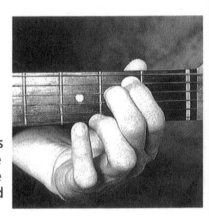

In addition to the doubled root and fifth (E and B, respectively), the minor chord contains a third note (G). The *interval* between the root (E) and the third (G) gives this chord its minor quality.

57

Compare the basic spellings of an Em chord and an E5 power chord.

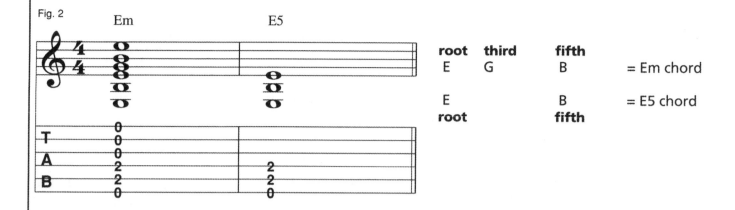

root	third	fifth	
E	G	B	= Em chord
E		B	= E5 chord
root		fifth	

INTERVALS

In analyzing the E minor chord, we have been looking at intervals. An interval is a group of two notes. They may be played melodically (one after the other) or harmonically (at the same time).
When an interval is played harmonically, it is called a *diad* (two-note chord). All of the two-note power chords we have learned are diads.

Every interval has two names, a number name and a quality name. The number name refers to the number of letter names apart the two notes are. In the E minor chord, E and G are 3 letter names apart.

E	F	**G**	A	B	C	D	A
1	2	**3**					

The interval from E up to G, then, is a *third* (minor third: m3)

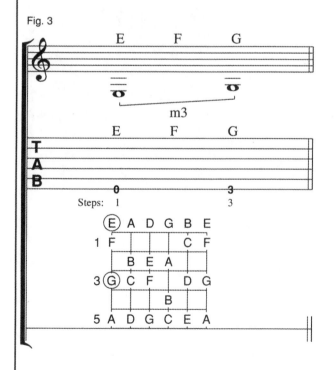

An interval's quality name relates to its melodic effect. We will look at this in more detail later. For now, realize that the note G is one half step lower than the G# note that is found in an E major scale. That half step difference makes the interval from E up to G a *minor third* (m3).

For practice, let's look at the interval between D and E.

D	E	F	G	A	B	C	D
1	2						

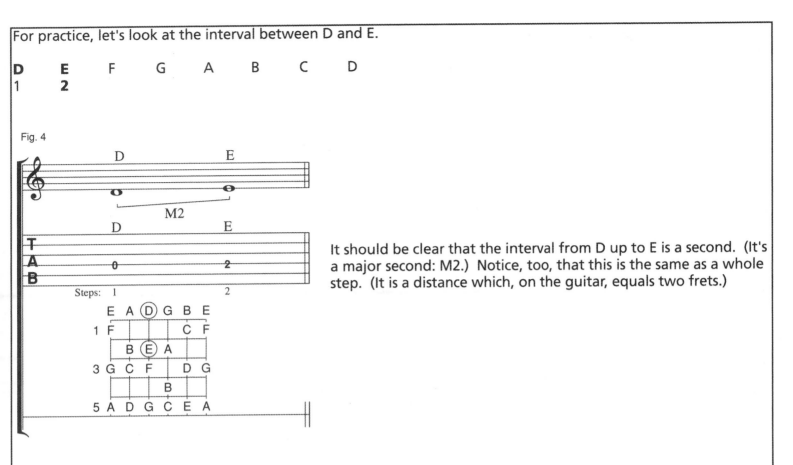

Fig. 4

It should be clear that the interval from D up to E is a second. (It's a major second: M2.) Notice, too, that this is the same as a whole step. (It is a distance which, on the guitar, equals two frets.)

Care must be taken when identifying intervals to refer to the direction of the distance between the notes.

The distance from D to E if you are moving up from the D is a major second (M2). (Figure 5)

The distance from D down to low E on the sixth string is much greater (it's a minor seventh: m7). (Figure 6)

The distance between the D and E on the fourth string is a major second whether you move up from D to E or down from E to D. This is true of any interval — the interval is the same regardless of which direction you move between the same exact two notes.

Fig. 5

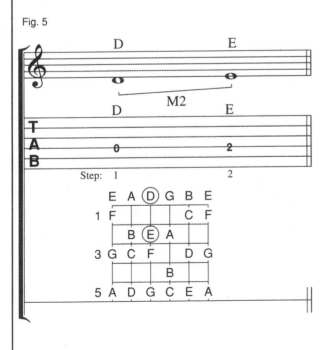

Fig. 6

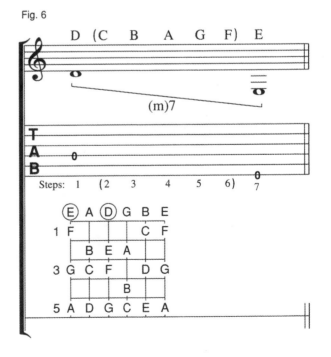

PLAYING TECHNIQUES

STRING BENDING

String bending is an important lead guitar technique that enables you to raise a fretted note's pitch smoothly and seamlessly, as if you were singing. It can also be used to approach "target" notes from below by bending up to them.

Let's get this technique under the fingers. Here's a bend on the 3rd string / 2nd fret from A to B. On the staff, the bend is represented by a bent line connecting the two notes. The note on the left is the unbent note; the note on the right is the bent note. The bend is indicated in the tablature by a curved arrow. The word "full" appearing directly above the arrow denotes a whole-step bend (A to B).

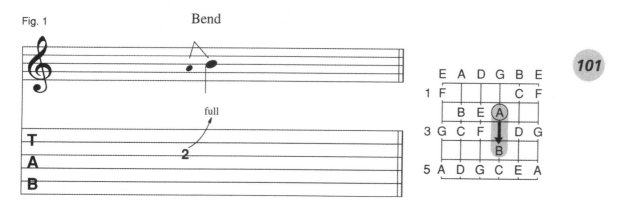

To execute the A to B bend:

1. Fret the A note on the 3rd string/2nd fret with your second finger.

2. Hook your thumb around the top of the fretboard. This will help anchor the hand as you bend the string.

3. Pick the string. You should hear an A note.

4. Using the tip of your second finger, push the string up toward the 4th strings to raise the pitch from A to B.

REINFORCED BEND FINGERING

Bending a string with a single finger can be an arduous task, especially in the lower area of the fretboard. It's much easier to bend a string with several fingers (reinforced fingering). The additional fingers provide you with more strength to push the string and enable you to control the pitch more easily (proper intonation). Try bending the A note up to B again, this time using the middle and index fingers to push the string. The additional finger is indicated below the tablature in parentheses.

Fig. 2

Reinforced Bends

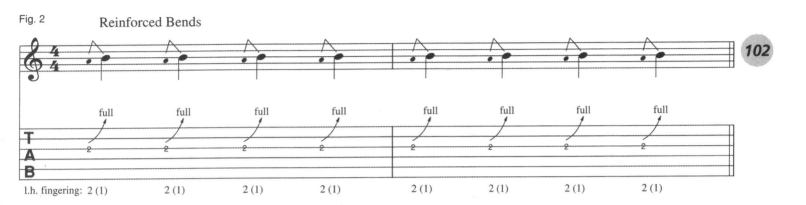

When executing the above bend, apply just enough push pressure to raise the pitch from A to B. Check your intonation by comparing the bent B note back-to-back with the open B note. The two pitches should be identical. Use your ears to determine exactly how much push pressure you'll need to apply.

Fig. 3

Now let's get into some musical applications of string bending. Here's a motif containing that A-to-B bend. It's an absolutely essential rock/blues lick. This is in eighth-note triplet rhythm. Each A-to-B bend should occupy one eighth-note's time. Repeat the motif (play it twice).

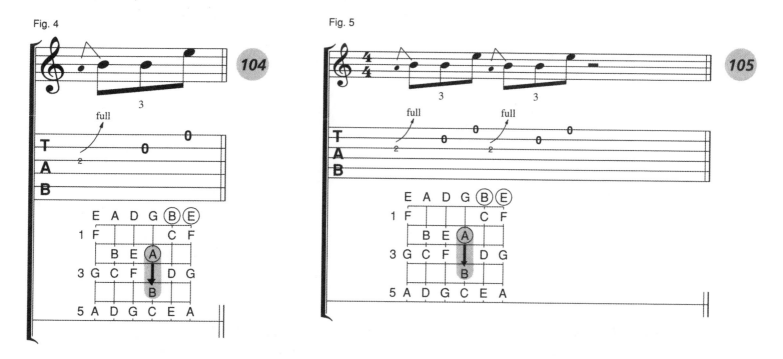

Next play it as an ostinato riff.

Now let's relate the motif sound to that of the Em chord. Play the Em chord, let it ring for one bar, then follow it with the ostinato lead riff from Figure 26.

By combining elements from the bend motif and our initial pentatonic motif, we can create a longer, riff-oriented rock / blues phrase. This is a familiar fixture in the solo approach of Chuck Berry, Angus Young and Slash as well as Chicago bluesmen like Otis Rush and Buddy Guy. The following example is a six-note figure in an eighth-note triplet rhythm. Bend the 3rd string with the index and middle fingers and fret the D note (2nd string / 3rd fret) with the ring finger.

Fig. 8

Let's try adapting the same riff pattern to a 16th-note rhythm. Listen to the way the feel of the line changes. The six-note motif now becomes rhythmically displaced.

Fig. 9

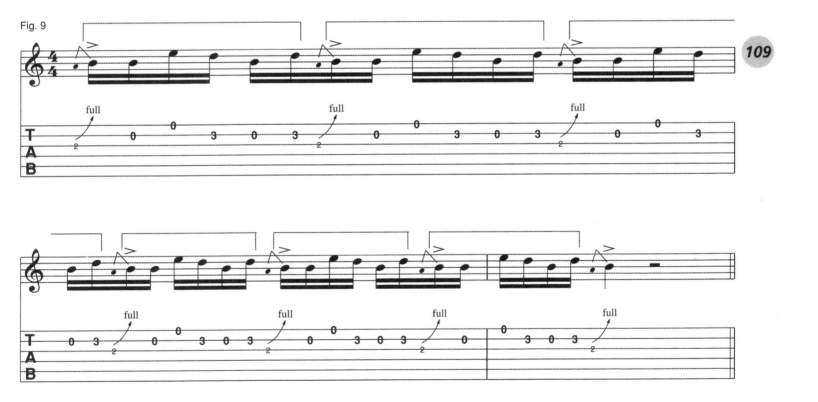

Here's another common blues/rock motif. This four-note figure employs the same type of bend as the last example, plus a string skip from the 3rd to the 1st string. Practice this maneuver slowly and concentrate on clean execution. Use alternate picking throughout.

Fig. 10

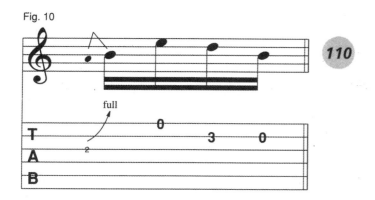

Now repeat the motif to create an ostinato riff.

Fig. 11

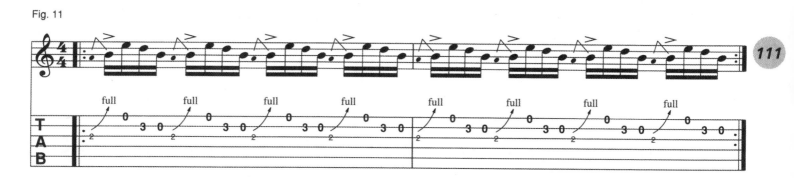

Let's go further in development and combine elements of the two previous motifs to create a longer phrase. Notice that the second bend is played in the space of two 16th notes, whereas the first bend is played in the space of one 16th note.

Fig. 12

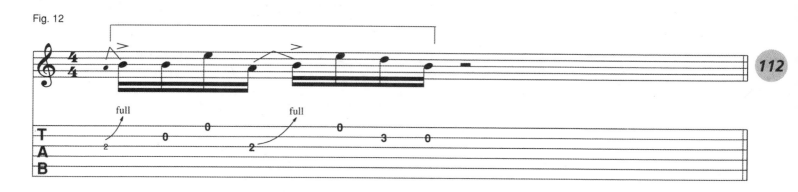

Now let's repeat the motif several times to create an ostinato riff.

Fig. 13

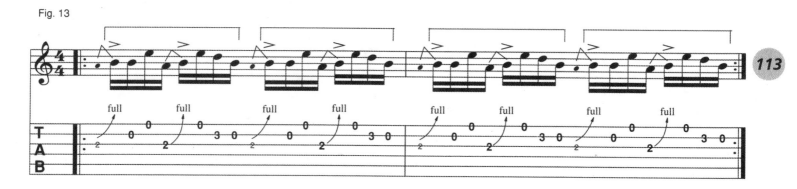